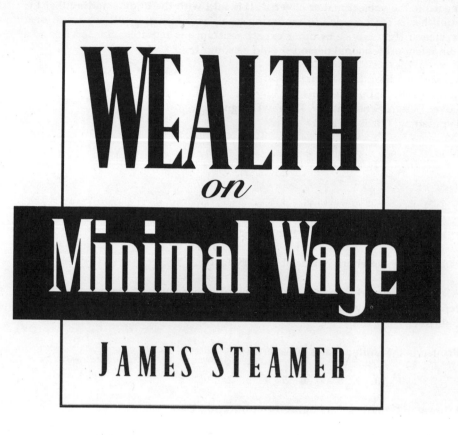

WEALTH
on
Minimal Wage

JAMES STEAMER

Dearborn
Financial Publishing, Inc.®

This publication is designed to provide accurate and authoritative information in regard to the subject matter covered. It is sold with the understanding that the publisher is not engaged in rendering legal, accounting, or other professional service. If legal advice or other expert assistance is required, the services of a competent professional person should be sought.

Managing Editor: Jack Kiburz
Interior Design: Lucy Jenkins
Cover Design: Scott Rattray, Rattray Design
Typesetting: Elizabeth Pitts

Printed in the United States of America

97 98 99 10 9 8 7 6 5 4 3 2

Library of Congress Cataloging-in-Publication Data

Steamer, James W.
    Wealth on minimal wage / James W. Steamer.
        p.   cm.
    Includes index.
    ISBN 0-7931-2240-6
    1. Consumer education—United States. 2. Finance, Personal—
United States. 3. Saving and thrift—United States. I. Title.
TX336.S74   1997
640'.42—dc20   96-36015
                                                             CIP

CONTENTS

PREFACE

Pablo Picasso once said, "I'd like to live like a poor man with lots of money." He sure had a point: Living this way places the "never enough" craving at bay. *Wealth on Minimal Wage* has been written to help you achieve financial freedom by providing you with hundreds of money-saving tips and an optimistic attitude toward money. It works. I know, I've been there. By cutting costs, saving money, and investing wisely, my wife and I have accumulated $250,000 in investments and home equity on less than $20,000 a year. Wealth *is* possible on a minimal wage, but it is *not* automatic. Begin by making a conscious decision to become resourceful and to understand your current and future needs. *Wealth on Minimal Wage* will show you how.

Acquiring a reasonable level of self-discipline will help you deal with your finances in productive ways. You will learn how to manage your money, how to understand the process to reach whatever goals you set, and how to stick with it. One healthy way to keep your momentum in achieving your goals is to place a big chart of your finances, showing all incoming and outgoing funds, on a prominent part of a wall that you see every day. As you learn to rearrange your finances for the better using this budget chart, you will see improvements; some right away and others over time. You may need to keep this chart for six months or a few years to receive sustained results. Don't allow excuses to get in the way. Whenever you catch yourself voicing something negative about your finances, stop, write down what you heard yourself say, place a bright red line through it, and attach it to the wall near your chart.

LIVE BY THESE TEN MONEY COMMANDMENTS

Wealth on Minimal Wage will help you live by the following commandments:

1. Implement *self-discipline* and *consistency* for the long-term.
2. Understand and calculate the risks of living—from risks to your physical, mental, and emotional health to investment risks.
3. Set *realistic* financial goals, taking into account your present income, expected future earnings, potential investment growth, and your age.
4. Get a grasp on what *enough* means to you, from the size of your home to the number of children you have, to the car you drive, to weighing the long-term value of your decisions against the possible stresses they will bring.
5. Legally pay the least amount of taxes that you can.
6. Achieve a *clear understanding* of the effect of compound interest and the time value of money.
7. Don't get swindled by scams and frauds, and report such activities to the authorities.
8. Get by with the *least amount of insurance* possible, making sure that you know the consequences of your decisions and are comfortable with them.
9. *Be responsible with credit*, use it to your advantage, and avoid it when not to your advantage.
10. Understand the value of *resourcefulness* in all areas of life and make it a habit.

Whether you are deeply in debt, a compulsive spender or saver, already have a good grasp on your finances, or merely want to become more aware of the potential of money to increase your comfort level with life in general, *Wealth on Minimal Wage* will fulfill your needs. My desire is that you begin to experience that money *can be* a joy and not a constant, nagging frustration. Through a variety of resourceful strategies and careful planning, you can have all the basics and more, regardless of what you earn. By viewing money as a means to providing present needs and pleasures, *and* as the conduit to future wealth, amazing achievements can be accomplished. In fact, once you've reached certain financial goals by using the tools of resourcefulness and delayed gratification, you will remain financially empowered for life, passing on this privilege to your future generations.

INTRODUCTION

Ten years ago, if anyone told me that one day I would write a book on how to become wealthy on lower wages, I would have considered this proposition to be absurd. First, I carried the assumption that anyone who earned low hourly wages for an extended period of time was resigning himself to a life of hardship, financial worries, and downward mobility. Second, I found that most books on personal finance did not offer practical advice that could be applied on a routine basis by low-wage earners. Most of the advice appeared to be tailored to those who earn far more, or have established employment with benefits, or are willing to significantly alter their lifestyles to what most view as sacrificing. Third, I figured that it takes a substantial income or inheritance, lottery winning, Wall Street knowledge, and perhaps a shrewd, unscrupulous personality to create wealth. Through experience I have proven that low to modest hourly wages do not have to translate into a commitment to living poor; that one can be a generous, law-abiding citizen without a great financial windfall and still have wealth; and that a book chock-full of exactly how any healthy working person may truly prosper can be written.

Yes, wealth on minimal wage is possible! It's not only an accomplishment of mine but also can be yours as well, no matter what your wage. Come on. What's the catch? Five bucks an hour simply can't create wealth. For many Americans, wealth means a nice home, decent cars, a big green lawn, cross-country vacations, sending the kids to the Ivy League, being debt-free, and having enough savings to leave money worries in the trash. Five bucks an hour hardly even pays the bills. Really?

Well, readers, my wife and I are living proof that wealth on minimal wage is possible without extreme hardship. We are in our late 30s with an 8-year-old son. Over the last ten years our total combined gross earned income averaged less than $20,000 a year, but during this period of time we have achieved the following:

- Purchased and completely furnished a comfortable suburban home, which is now valued at $110,000
- In addition to the $19,000 down payment for the home, we have accumulated over $170,000 in savings
- Purchased three dependable cars with cash
- Paid off a $5,000 student loan, eliminating all nonmortgage debt
- Have enough cash invested in our son's account to comfortably cover his college education when the time arrives
- Covered the cost of a high-quality preschool program full-time for our son
- Continue to save over 25 percent of our income
- Enjoy cross-country trips and are planning some international ones as well
- Have the expectation to retire or work by choice before the age of 50
- Hope to be free of our $50,000 home mortgage in the not-too-distant future

I don't doubt that I have provoked the curiosity of many readers, regardless of their financial status. The main purpose of this book is to fully respond to this curiosity. When confronted with the fact that our net worth exceeds all of our earned income over the previous ten years, a couple of respected national finance magazines reacted in disbelief until their staff viewed our past financial records. One magazine flatly refused to believe it, saying "Your figures don't add up." After that, I have become even more committed to placing this information into the hands of all who can benefit—everyone earning from $10,000 to $100,000 a year. And certainly an IRS audit in which the auditor, when seeing our savings compared with our income, said, "What do you live on, beans and peanut butter?", left an indelible memory. Then came the married couple interviewed on television who cast doubts about the affordability of raising more than one child on their $100,000-a-year-plus income. Meanwhile, a coworker of mine, earning $6 an hour, was a happily married mother of six with a husband earning about the same wage. They owned their home, had some savings, and were nearly debt-free. Such observations fueled my determination to explore and understand the full range of human struggle and mastery in the world of money.

WHO IS JIM STEAMER?

While completing my liberal arts degree in the early 1980s with the expectation of locating employment that had reasonable advancement potential, I had a part-time business selling my color photographs. My fiancee, Kathleen, had just completed an internship assisting the elderly poor in preparing their wills. Though as a child I persevered to achieve goals and was careful how I spent money, operating my own business helped me see how money works. And having my brother try to convince my father to buy shares of McDonald's stock around the age of 12 did not hurt. (There are times when it pays to listen to your children!) Shortly after graduating we moved south to Austin, Texas, leaving Massachusetts winters and higher costs of living behind us to face a new adventure. From the photo business begun with $50 three years earlier, I had saved about $25,000.

Like many college graduates, we faced a competitive job market with a need for specialists in business, law, medicine, engineering, and high tech. We found ourselves primarily employable in service-oriented, clerical, and manufacturing jobs. We have worked at an assortment of over 50 jobs in the past 12 years in order to achieve financial security, satisfaction, and wealth. Our hourly wages began at the 1983 minimum wage of $3.35 per hour (less than I earned years before as a busboy and dishwasher). Here is a sampling of the jobs from those years:

- Serving as caretakers for a wealthy older couple for about $1,000 a month plus free rent and utilities
- Clerical and light industrial temping for banks, insurance companies, printing centers, and state agencies for $4 to $5 per hour
- Assembling awnings and bug killing lamps for $4 per hour
- Counting and testing integrated circuits for $3.75 per hour

- Cutting large rags into small rags for $5 per hour—the most dismal work of my life, I think
- Videotape duplication for $6.50 per hour
- Driving a delivery van for $5 per hour
- Conducting retail store inventory for $4.25 per hour
- Substitute teaching in the public schools for $40 a day
- House painting for about $5 per hour
- Waiting tables for about $6.50 per hour, including tips
- Cleaning houses for $5 per hour
- Loading 250-pound bundles of copper pipe into trucks in a 110-degree warehouse for $5.50 per hour. (I'll let you guess why I quit this job.)
- Stuffing over 2,000,000 antistatic electrical grounding straps one at a time into envelopes in a 40-degree warehouse heated by roaring, foul-smelling kerosene heaters, for $6 per hour

I now work in a friendly, comfortable environment verifying/confirming orders by telephone while writing and pursuing my financial consulting business. Kathleen is employed as a teacher in our public schools. Our earned household income has now certainly exceeded $20,000 a year. We learned to accept unrewarding work while always pursuing better opportunities through job seeking and further education. However, we discovered through earning less money and carefully saving and investing that we could live on less and live comfortably. We now have more time and energy to pursue our hobbies, travel, and share activities with our son. Therefore, we feel more relaxed about the future and well prepared to face the prospect of retirement.

A main part of this book consists of an extensive and concise list of money-saving methods we have used, may still be using, may use in our future, or may be of practical value to others. The most important message conveyed to everyone is that with the information presented here, nearly all people can enjoy the rewards of living well on less.

Before jumping directly into the tips on wealth accumulation, I want to present a discussion about money and wealth. I view wealth as being broader than just high digits in a bank account. It is my hope that you will implement many of the principles provided here, substantially increase your net worth, and become more satisfied with your life as a whole. Additionally, I anticipate that your awareness of the responsibility money carries and its importance and potential will be greatly enhanced. Of course, I realize that you may not have the same financial goals and dreams that I have. However, this book will assist you in defining your dream and fulfilling it in a comprehensive and friendly manner. You will learn how to figure the real worth of money you earn, spend less while increasing the quality of your life, get out of debt, understand where to safely invest money, and reduce your taxes.

CHAPTER 1

Setting Your
Financial Goals

The time spent applying the advice presented in this book will consume only about an hour a week or less as you become accustomed to new and satisfying ways of dealing with your money. The most challenging part may be changing your *attitudes* about finances. Hopefully, the variety of solutions I offer here will trigger some positive changes and stimulate your interest in finance in general. As much as considerable information on money is understandably boring to many people, I hope that your own potential to create more wealth than you ever dreamed possible will soon become clear and that you will keep reading.

Wisdom on Wealth

Wealth accumulation requires considerable *determination* at the individual level.

Becoming wealthy is not a group activity. Wealth accumulation requires considerable *determination* at the individual level. As you use these techniques and become wealthier, you will be more self-confident and eliminate peer pressure and self-consciousness. You will be able to ignore those nasty comments about your rusting '83 Toyota and feel good about quietly sacking away $350 a month with clear expectations of becoming financially independent. While a new car owner may feel proud and happy enjoying the comforts of a new car, the Toyota owner may be in a more empowered position financially and will probably buy his or her next car in cash.

Following styles and the behaviors of others rarely leads to wealth in my experience. Those who swim against the social current have a hard time being accepted if they reveal their full determination to gain greater control of their lives. Getting control means increasing your financial position relative to that of others of similar income, status, and background. It's a fine line. There are those who will label you as "selfish" and "greedy." And it is often mistakenly assumed that those who wish to accumulate wealth and become self-empowered are only out for number one. Remember that you work hard for your money and have the right to do as you please with it—within reason.

Be selective to whom you choose to reveal your finances and financial values, especially during the early stages of wealth building. Some of your actions will speak for themselves, however. I have found that showing my own attitudes and goals in personal finance has often not gone over well in social situations. I have been labeled "miserly" and "cheap" by some, and have been respected by others. At the same time, skeptics are curious about how to move up the ladder of success on "menial" wages. I have seen jealous parents who struggled much of their lives withdraw their life savings because they feel their children are doing so well that they won't need an inheritance. And, on hearing that I am more financially prudent, some have tried to convince me to change, explaining that "I could be run over by a truck or become terminally ill tomorrow, so live only for today." Those who expend a lot of effort worrying about the minuscule downside risks in life may never relish the upside pleasures over the years.

Your best answer to those who are unsupportive or jealous is to demonstrate your satisfaction in life through your *actions* and avoid the topic of finances unless specifically asked. One day when you are without a mortgage, don't need to use credit because you pay for everything in cash, send your children to the college of their choice, spend summers touring foreign lands, retire early, or work for an outside employer because you *want* to, your actions will communicate better than your words ever will. For those you trust, share a common financial philosophy, or you wish to teach, exchanging information may benefit all parties involved. I have plenty of experience to back this up.

Dare to be unique! Tap into your unrealized talents and don't talk yourself out of getting the skills needed for a good job. As the old saying goes, the sky is the limit! Ignore movements, trends, and fashions that are designed primarily to keep people buying. Give up fear of embarrassment or criticism. Your self-assurance will grow and great rewards will be forthcoming.

Who can become financially independent early on in life? Everyone who earns money can. Unfortunately, being in a position to retire early from paid employment is something most people only occasionally dream about. Many resent those who do retire early. They tend to believe that if one is not working for a paycheck, then one is not being productive, and therefore is living at the expense of others who do work hard. This assumption holds little weight, for those who live from investments leave their money invested in the economy, helping to provide more jobs and lower debt.

Wisdom on Wealth

You will soon realize that you can be the master of money, rather than let money dictate your life decisions on a continuing basis.

You will soon realize that you can be the master of money, rather than let money dictate your life decisions on a continuing basis. When your relationship with money becomes properly structured in a manner that maximizes its usefulness to you, the chances of money increasing your level of satisfaction rises immensely. The debate about whether money makes one happier may continue indefinitely, but the issue at hand is not money itself, but how people cope with it. A hefty stack of 20-dollar bills can bring about greater satisfaction to one person than a stack of 100-dollar bills may to another.

Unless they were fortunate enough to land great-paying jobs early on, or have money from other sources, could people in *previous* generations live the American dream soon after finishing school? Generally *not*, even though in those days, a decent home and car cost so much less. My parents did not enter into that "dream lifestyle" until they reached their 40s. Of course, World War II delayed some people from becoming settled into their work and family lives. Today, many people achieve a comfortable standard of living before they reach the age of 30, especially couples who both work and share the major expense of housing. This change occurred in the mid-1970s, when it became more common for women to have higher-paying jobs. Now with two people working, each contributing more than $40,000 to the household income, this exclusive, though not rare, group live a very comfortable lifestyle.

According to 1995 Census Bureau data, annual household gross earned incomes of more than $50,000 belong to about 10 percent of the U.S. population and those with incomes of $100,000 drop to less than 5 percent. Certainly the unequal distribution of wealth is causing much discontent among large numbers of people as some continue to earn more in minutes than others do in years. Many people have resigned themselves to a life of struggling to pay bills and accepting the mediocrity of a routine of money in, money out, money in, money out. I prove that such a life must be lived this way only by those who choose to. Jobs that bring in very comfortable levels of income dependably are less abundant and often further schooling is necessary to have a better chance at getting them. The dream is still within reach for all of us, however, whether you earn $13,000 a year in a low-status service job or $50,000+ a year as a professional.

You have a fixed amount of *time* to spend in your life, normally 70 to 90 years. Human happiness occurs when you are able to spend an adequate percentage of this time engaging in stimulating, challenging, and pleasurable activities. Only you can define what an adequate percentage is and what is most rewarding.

CHILDHOOD LIMITATIONS

Most of us grow into our teen years with an astounding ignorance of money. You probably had a piggy bank as a child, a small weekly allowance, and a passbook savings account, and you may have learned the basics of handling a checking account. Your parents may have made references to saving for college and, once you obtained a job, had you pay for haircuts, dental cleanings, and some clothing. In some less-affluent homes, employed teenagers were expected to chip in for essentials such as food and utility bills. Alternative places to save money other than the local bank were rarely acknowledged. I don't recall that reading the business section of the newspaper was a high priority in my family. We all learned that essentials must be paid for first, nonessentials and pleasures later, and perhaps a little something should be put away for a rainy day. Financial and economic education were less important in the past because the promise of dependable financial security through education and employment was nearly a given, if one possessed just a modest amount of motivation. Clearly, we now live in different times.

While certainty about our financial future seems to have faded, our desire to live the American dream hasn't died. For most people, the American dream is home ownership, comfortable and dependable transportation, the creation of offspring, freedom to travel, eating out at least a couple of times a month, nice clothing, a green lawn, being able to save something for the future, and *enough income* to support it all. Have you arrived when you have all of these? Not necessarily. But financial security can help to eliminate some of the negative stress in our lives that seems to zap us of so much energy.

HIGH RETURNS FOR EVERYONE

My father could not simply dial a toll-free number to a mutual fund, set up electronic bank account draft plans, or invest in a tax-deferred, deductible IRA during his younger years. Today, a six-year-old child can invest as little as $25 a month, take on the same risk/reward ratios, and average 12 percent annual returns, which only the wealthy used to have access to. Even though everything appears to be so costly, now it is actually far easier to accumulate wealth than ever before. In fact, if that six-year-old kept on investing only $25 a month until the age of 65, assuming a tax-free annual average return of 12 percent, he or she would have amassed nearly a *million dollars!* It is downright bizarre for a six-year-old to be contemplating wealth at the age of 65, but parents can quietly do their part. Of course, saving for college may be a higher priority, because young adults can create their own retirement funds when they begin working. It is certainly intriguing to note that just $1,000 placed in such a high-return investment at birth could conceivably generate more from investment income without dipping into principal than all that child might collect in Social Security, if the account were permitted to grow tax-free for 65 years. Maybe the federal government will demonstrate some creative options of this type to help solve the coming Social Security dilemma.

You must become your own money manager. Nearly everyone would like to save some extra cash, but it always seems that there is rarely any left over. Few people deny that they want to have some savings, or better still, dependable income from their savings, or even better still, enough investment income to become completely financially independent. This is all possible, even on minimum wage.

Wisdom on Wealth

You must become your own money manager.

Here are several examples of excuses that people use for not taking control of their finances:

- "I am too old to begin now."
- "I don't care about having lots of things. I just want to be comfortable."
- "I am only in my 20s. Why should I think about retirement?"
- "I am too busy to get into investing. Besides, I don't have money savvy anyway."
- "The stock market is far too risky. My grandfather lost everything in it."
- "I couldn't even pass algebra. How to you expect me to amass a fortune?"
- "Bills are waiting for my paycheck at the end of every month. How do you expect me to save and invest?"
- "I am not a handyman so I could never fix up an old house properly. Besides, hassling with renters and taking on the responsibility of property ownership is simply too overwhelming."
- "All I have is here and now. I may not be here tomorrow so I am enjoying life *now!*"

People use these excuses because they lack information and confidence, are insecure about managing money, or are just plain lazy. Access to the financial world is now many times easier than algebra and certainly far less difficult or intimidating than in comparatively recent times.

GOAL SETTING

Whether completing school, climbing a mountain, losing weight, finding work you want, or saving money for an intended purpose, goal setting is *the key* to success. Unfortunately, many of us are not born goal setters. For these people I suggest setting a series of smaller, more manageable goals so achieving big goals that can initially appear overwhelming may be accomplished with less frustration. Some people simply live each day with little concern or interest in the future, while others can hardly let a moment pass without calculating its long-term value. Neither the extreme of routine procrastination nor stoically driving yourself 16 hours a day to reach goals are healthy ways to live over the *long-term*. Without giving yourself a solid push during certain periods, however, you may not get the results you desire. Completing this book while working at least 50 hours a week, still squeezing in time to be a husband and father, learning Windows 95 while divorcing my IBM Selectric II, and still getting enough sleep has *me* in the 16-hour-day mode. Working this hard certainly is not meant to be a ten-*year* state of living, but for ten *months* this is what it takes to responsibly accomplish these goals. Can you muster up the determination and self-discipline not only to set goals, but also to accomplish what must get done to achieve them? Can you realize that the hard work involved in getting what you want may be worth the short-term sacrifice? We all have the willpower to create great, exciting, and rewarding accomplishments. What else are we here for? The following four-step plan will enable you to get started and keep your financial life moving forward.

STEP ONE

Reach for your willpower and change your attitude. Instead of viewing budgets and inexpensive alternatives as burdensome, take pride in the knowledge that you now can make the money you earn go farther, and that you know exactly where and how your money is spent. Rather than envying the person who bought a $46 shirt, feel proud that you bought the same shirt in near-perfect condition for $5 and earmarked the other $41 for other purchases or savings. Noticing your increased savings from your paycheck will provide you with the first hints of self-empowerment.

STEP TWO

Identify all predictable income, most of which probably comes from an employer's paycheck. Always try to advance yourself at your present place of employment, upgrade your skills, and attempt to locate better work. Also, determine how you can downsize your living costs without giving up much (see the budget chart on pages 10–11). Corporations are *improving* themselves by downsizing. So can you! If your living expenses still equal or exceed what you take home from one job, then do one of three things: (1) Get a second job (doing so may be only temporary to reach a goal such as eliminating debt); (2) work overtime at your regular job, if possible; (3) downsize/reorganize your lifestyle further. For example, you might work alternating shifts with your spouse to care for a young child, rather than paying a fortune for child care, or carpool with two people that, at a dollar a day from each, would pay for all of your gasoline.

Even if you are qualified for a $50,000, high-tech job with every known benefit, these days you may have to work, at least temporarily, in a field or position for which you are overqualified, and for much less money than you expected or are used to. Chances are, if you are stuffing envelopes, telemarketing, or flipping burgers with four or more years of college behind you, you are not alone! Just be persistent and determined. See Chapter 3 for complete details on employment and alternative income sources.

Wisdom on Wealth

No matter how little my income is, it will always be greater than my expenses.

STEP THREE

Start setting your financial goals *now*. Every day that passes in which you don't is *costing you money*. A good rule to remember is that financial goals often are reached more through what people *save* than what they earn. It may be great to have a high salary, but the person earning far less may become financially independent sooner, by employing knowledge and self-discipline. How realistic your particular goals are depends on your age, earnings, present debt load, saving capacity, and tolerance for short-term risk. Once you begin living by this next sentence, the first stone of your financial foundation will have been laid. No matter how little my income is, it will always be greater than my expenses. For many people I recommend writing this down in bold print and taping the paper to the bathroom mirror. Keep another copy in your check register and another covering your credit and automatic teller machine (ATM) cards. Post-It notes work well for this purpose.

STEP FOUR

Create a worksheet with several columns (see sample on pages 10–11) as follows: Label the first column "present expenses," which includes every penny that you spend each month, regardless of its purpose. This is to be done without *any* changes in your lifestyle. The second column is "fixed expenses." It includes only those costs from the first column that can't be easily altered such as rent, car payment, mortgage cost, and basic service charges for utilities and telephone. In the third column, list expenses that can be altered or eliminated. And in column four, "extra money," estimate how much you are able to cut or increase (by paying off high-interest debt, for example) amounts from column three. In column five, list all income from predictable sources, and in column six, list your financial goals for the short, medium, and long-term. I generally consider short to mean under 5 years, medium to mean 5 to 15 years, and long to be more than 15 years. The purpose of creating this system is to clarify exactly how much money is coming in, how much is going out, where it is going, and how changes can be implemented for the better. Initially, creating a budget may feel painful and mundane, but doing so is the first active step you are taking to change some deeply ingrained habits. Depending on your level of financial troubles, withdrawal symptoms, comparable to those who are no longer chemically dependent, may be experienced by some.

As much as you may wish to promptly start improving your finances, it is normally best to wait one month while you continue to live as you have—keeping an accurate expense diary, down to the penny. And don't forget to average out bills that you pay less frequently than once a month, such as car insurance and registration, income and property taxes, etc. For example, if your car insurance premium is $350 every six months or $700 a year, this averages out to $58.34 per month. The third column is critical, for this is where you can feel as though you are getting a raise by reducing your expenses. You must ask yourself whenever you spend money if you can do without the purchase, delay it, or buy it for less. You also must question what methods of payment such as cash, checks, or credit cards make you more aware of spending your money. Do you enjoy the feeling of paying in cash or by money order with the immediate relief that something is paid in full? Or do you cope better by adding and subtracting entries in a check register? Perhaps you'd prefer to own the item for a month until your credit-card bill arrives?

Budget Worksheet

Present Expenses	Fixed Expenses	How Reduced
Mortgage/Rent		
First Car Payment		
Second Car Payment		
Health Insurance		
Groceries		
Eating Out		
Child Care		
Child Support		
Utilities		
Telephone		
Auto Insurance		
Gasoline		
Auto Maintenance		
Income Taxes		
Property Taxes		
Clothing		
Doctor		
Dental		
Charity		
Life Insurance		
Entertainment		
Home Repairs		
Vacation		
Personal Care		
Credit Card		
Miscellaneous		

Budget Worksheet

Extra Money	Fixed Income	Goals

Time is another important factor to budget along with money. You occasionally may need to estimate your earnings from various types of work against other time-consuming activities, which may have a chance of earning more money or bringing other satisfaction your way. Is it worth working an extra job to pay off a debt sooner, while giving up some time at home in the short term? These choices can be made only at the individual level based on your particular goals, personality, and lifestyle.

Everyone's finances vary considerably, so you should customize the sample worksheet to your individual needs. Whether you live on $10,000 or more than $100,000 a year, certain expenses can be reduced to reach various goals. I believe you will discover that skimming off 10 to 20 percent of your income or more, in some cases, is much less difficult than you anticipated initially. As you read through this book, make your own budget chart or modify the one supplied here to fit your circumstances. The more time you have on your side, the brighter your prospects, so get started ASAP! Finding "new money" that you did not realize you had available can truly be exciting. In fact, you can even make a game out of budgeting and reward yourself as certain goals are reached—even if you have to *spend money* to do so!

Many highly successful and financially independent individuals have acquired their wealth by practicing long-term stability and investing, resourcefulness, and simplicity as a way of life. A large portion of affluent people had surprisingly humble beginnings. This is largely what determines whether they will maintain a healthy perspective on money. Before I present my list of wealth-building strategies, it is crucial to rethink and reevaluate the role money plays in your life. I can tell you how to become a millionaire on less than $10 per hour, but first you must examine how much added satisfaction you will acquire from the pricey possessions wealth can buy. Or can you see becoming wealthy as providing you with empowerment, freedom, or other intangibles? Will you discover that having more zeros past the first whole number in your bank account is actually rewarding? You may experience the startling revelation that having *less* of what money buys in material terms can mean *more* satisfaction within a range. From the young age at which we realize that money has the power to provide material pleasures, to adulthood when we put forth effort to receive money, and to our long-awaited older years, when we depend on money to maintain a satisfying lifestyle, we must come to terms with the pivotal role money plays in our lives.

CHAPTER 2

Understanding Your
Money Personality

The ability to *achieve* the American dream has become an established institution. Although I am using the word *American* here, this dream is not exclusive to just those living in an industrialized nation. Everyone wants to achieve what can be summed up in three words: *security, comfort,* and *choices.* People want to have the income to support comfortable housing in a safe area, be able to have children without financial hardship, pursue personal interests and travel, plan for a secure retirement, and obtain work they find rewarding and dependable. Basically, people want more *control* of their lives, and money has the potential to provide much of this dream.

A working person's average income has not kept pace with the costs of supporting most households. Why? Because the cost of housing itself has increased. Because of the greater work opportunities for women in the past few decades, more double-income households exist. And because working couples are able and willing to pay more for a house than single-income families, housing costs have risen. In addition, quality housing for the American family is stretching the budgets of today's two-income households, especially when the increased costs of utilities, health care, transportation, and child care are taken into account.

> ## Wisdom on Wealth
>
> Only when our needs and wants can be adjusted to cost less than our incomes provide can we ease the stress on our budgets.

No matter what the obstacles are—high housing costs, lost or low-paying jobs, single parenthood, or a medical mishap—the basic ingredients of the dream are still possible, although obtaining them may present more creative challenges. If you have a general knowledge of economics and the potential of money, the American dream can still be yours.

In fact, with the right money knowledge, people can climb up the economic ladder even farther and acquire greater financial freedom than ever before. Even if you're earning the minimum wage, a sizable portion of a person's life can be spent living the dream, as we will see in later chapters. Regardless of present economic conditions, this continues to be a fine period of history in which to be alive.

THE DREAM VERSUS YOUR DREAM

Before leaping into a diehard pursuit of *the* dream, you must examine what *your* dream is. What are the highest values and needs that *truly add* to your satisfaction in life? To what degree does owning various material possessions add or subtract from this satisfaction? Is it worth the effort and time of having a second job or living within one or two paychecks of homelessness to maintain a ten-room home? Would it be more satisfying to live in a smaller place, not need the extra job, be able to live on less than a take-home salary, be responsible for less, and have more free time?

Does that new dream car make you feel better? Or do the high payments, maintenance costs, insurance, taxes, and registration renewal expenses merely keep you dreaming? Do personal computers actually save time or money, provide you with the pleasures you expected, or help keep you living from paycheck to paycheck, because of their initial high costs, accessories, and additional upgrading costs? Does having the maximum insurance on your life, health, home, liability, car, and any number of other things really provide you with true *peace* of mind or financial *stress* of mind? How many children can you enjoy without having to work so much, and, therefore, lose quality time with them? Just how high a tower can you build full of houses, cars, boats, insurance, vacations, shopping sprees, children, college educations, and 50- to 60-hour workweeks to pay for it all, before it becomes top-heavy with negative stress?

Unfortunately, many people measure their self-worth by the size of their paycheck when what they do all those hours to receive it should ideally bring more satisfaction than the money. When people learn to become more content with their work and budget their money and time more efficiently, there will be great benefits to all.

Wisdom on Wealth

Who can become financially independent early on in their lives? Everyone able to earn money can!

Certainly I hope that you will soon realize that you can be the master of money rather than letting money dictate your life decisions on a continuing basis. When your relationship with money becomes properly structured, the chance of money increasing your happiness rises immensely, whether you earn $13,000 or more than $50,000 a year. The sooner you can begin using the ideas and advice presented here and stay with it, the better. It is simple for me to tell you how you can turn $40 a month into more than a million dollars. But how many of us will become conscious enough of our money personalities to drop negative habits, trust other and new ideas, and make use of them?

Wisdom on Wealth

Can you identify your threshold of having enough of what money can buy, beyond which no further meaning is added to your life?

Only you can decide where your level of financial and material comfort, security, freedom, or power in dollar amounts and material goals lies. Do you believe the statement, "When I earn more, I spend more," thus experiencing the same frustration as the man who stayed in debt no matter how high his salary became? Certainly there is nothing wrong with changing your lifestyle and goals *to some extent* if you are fortunate enough to find a $17-per-hour job after living on $6 an hour. But if your goals change to reflect each pay raise over the years, you may never reach total prosperity. You will merely want $25 an hour when you get the $17-an-hour job. This type of thinking will trap you indefinitely. However, if the $17-an-hour worker lived on $10 an hour after moving up from $6 an hour and invested the other $7 (less after taxes), enormous rewards for this discipline would not be too many years off.

Finding out at what point we have *enough*, in which our lives are balanced with regard to our material needs and wants, is a question I will explore from several angles. I believe that when people can define, understand, and accept realistic and comfortable parameters for their financial/material needs, they will be closer to immense personal fulfillment, assuming their health is good and their companionship needs are being met.

Our bonding with material objects travels through life from the baby bottle to our first bicycle, from TV and stereo to cars and houses. As a consumer, I have purchased numerous items that have enhanced my life with increased comfort, decor, and convenience. But the question always arises: "Do we place the acquisition of material goods at such high priority that we no longer are able to experience the simple pleasures of everyday life?"

TIME AND ENERGY HAVE THEIR PRICE

Many of us wake up and drive to work with the familiar and distressing thought of "another day, another dollar." Do we find ourselves spending a considerable amount of time and energy preparing, thinking, attending, commuting, and unwinding from our work? We indeed spend a considerable amount of time and energy preoccupied and involved with our jobs. If you include all job-related time and energy consumed outside of working hours, you will find this time and energy no longer is yours to enjoy, nor does it accurately reflect your true human worth. Because you probably will never be compensated sufficiently for all this effort, you must decide at some point just how much time and energy you want to commit to your job. If you place a high value on all your time and energy both on and off the job, you will be able to experience greater job satisfaction in the present, prioritizing where to place your efforts.

For now, you must come to terms with what you earn and assess the full potential of your paycheck and how it affects your buying decisions. For example, let's assume that after paying your monthly bills you have finally saved an extra $1,000. This $1,000 could be spent on a new video camera. The same new camera can be purchased on sale at another store for $800. The identical camera, used but in perfect condition, is available for $450. If you decide to rent a camera occasionally, it may cost $25 a day. There is also the friendly neighbor who may be willing to lend you the camera on an as-needed basis, at no cost.

Wisdom on Wealth

When was the last time you explored *all* your options before making an impulsive purchase? This one simple action can save you more money than any single budgeting trick I can think of.

To find out how much time, money, and energy it consumes to acquire $1,000 simply divide $1,000 by your hourly wage to get the total number of hours you spent. An individual who earns $6.25 per hour would have to engage in paid employment at this rate for 160 hours to buy the camera brand new, not taking into account the employer withholding taxes or sales tax on the camera that add on more time and energy to the equation. To buy it on sale for $800 would cost 128 hours, and purchasing it used for $450 would consume just 72 hours of time.

If you decide to invest the $1,000, the investment returns could pay for renting the camera a few times a year—and still leave *you* in control of the $1,000. Should you decide to pay full price for the camera, ask yourself why. Perhaps you are a professional videographer who justifies the cost in peace of mind or a typical consumer who feels you are getting more because you're paying more. By understanding your deepest emotional and material needs, and placing a high value on your time and energy, you will become more comfortable with choosing the less costly methods. This type of thinking will lead you on a path to greater freedom, independence, and control of your destiny.

MONEY AND PERSONAL FULFILLMENT

Obviously, if we spend *less money* to have what we want, then we can have *more freedom* to enjoy many other pleasures. Many marriages fall apart primarily because couples believe that each must work around the clock to acquire material possessions. Do they really want these possessions enough to severely restrict their time to relax, to spend with each other, or with children, family, and friends? In such families where the parents are so consumed by career and material advancement, children are being deprived of necessary bonding and attention. Children need parents' *time* more than what money buys, as several respected studies now show. For example, I recall cutting up and sanding down some scrap lumber an employer gave me into wooden play blocks while on a work break. These free blocks have provided my son with as much or more enjoyment as expensive toys, leaving the money we saved to be earmarked for other things and offsetting my modest salary. Dividends from not having this expense can be recreated by these free blocks for generations to come.

HAVING ENOUGH AND DEFLATION

If one has been living on a given income and after a number of years of accumulating enough housing, garden, transportation, clothes, appliances, decor, gadgets, is eating well, and providing enough for the household, where is the money *now* going that was being used to purchase these things, most of which last for many years? Once my new central air-conditioning system was installed, it will not require a several-thousand-dollar replacement for more than 15 years. A house can hold only so much furniture and I need only one socket wrench set. Once long-term and permanent purchases are paid for, the cost of living for many households can go *down* and money that was paying for these things now can be spent on luxuries such as travel, hobbies, and investments. For those who are parents, when children reach the age when they no longer need day care, this major expense will be eliminated as well. If you have a mortgage, the cost of living can drop even further or at least help offset some college costs when it is paid off. The experience of *deflation* or at least *no inflation* will vary depending on individual circumstances, but it can be enjoyed with prudent planning.

THE ECONOMICS OF LIFE CHART

This chart is a simplified version of the potential economic lifeline all working people can follow. You may fill in your figures to suit your situation. I have estimated wage increases conservatively for the reader's benefit. Hopefully, your wages will rise faster than this, but it's best to not assume this. Regarding expenses, I am going by my own recommendations of living on at least 10 percent less than after-tax wages. The peak in the middle represents the greatest expenses such as raising a family and paying off a mortgage, and the downward slope shows the deflationary trend, when children are on their own, mortgages are paid off, and perhaps an inheritance occurs. As savings accumulate, potential investment income from savings grows until working for a wage becomes an option and financial independence is achieved. As an extra hedge of security, you should wait until your investment income equals 20 percent or more than what is actually needed to permit you to invest a portion of savings in longer-term, higher-yielding growth investments.

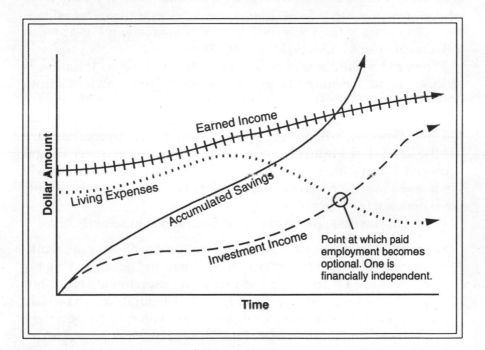

THE REALITY OF INFLATION

As long as money has existed, there has been a tendency toward inflation. One of several contributing factors is human nature—the desire to have more, often at the expense of borrowing to do so. As more money is borrowed and loaned out, the supply of money increases, which continues to fuel inflation. As the population grows and technology advances, more people need and want more, which is another factor. Low interest rates can be another major influence for the lower they are, the easier it is for businesses and consumers to borrow money. Printing too much money also can play a role. Printing more cash devalues its relative worth so that more will be needed to purchase the same amount of products and services. Similarly, increasing the availability of money through credit also affects inflation.

During your lifetime the annual inflation rate has paralleled or been somewhat lower than interest rates—around 6 percent per year on the average. This statement only applies to the United States and a few other select countries. More recently, inflation has been even lower. We are fortunate because in some countries inflation rates of hundreds of percent per year are typical. I hope we never experience what happened in Hungary from July 1945 to July of the following year when inflation jumped by 1,366,521,740,000,000 percent!

Experiences like these sound absurd, but as long as inflation is strictly *nominal*, meaning that proportions of money at all levels from the consumer to business and government remain the same, the impact is not significant. It takes no more effort to carry $100 bills around than $10 bills. However, when inflation is *real* we feel it, for proportions are *not* the same and gradually more parts of the economic chain get squeezed. When more dollars are required to sustain the same lifestyle while one's income remains unchanged or increases at a slower rate, we experience the effects of real inflation.

What can you do to protect yourself against real inflation?

- First of all don't buy the largest house you can afford even if others suggest it might be a "good investment and generate a big tax deduction." Of course, good real estate investments exist, but your primary residence should not be keeping you financially strapped. If you can afford only $1,000 a month for a house or rent payment, find an alternative for $700 to $800. Then take the extra $200 to $300 and invest it in a place that appreciates at a faster rate than the inflation rate. These investments are not hard to find and can rise at two or three times the recent rates of inflation, as you will see in Chapter 11.

- Second, never pay full price for anything, a task not hard to accomplish as you'll see later on.
- Third, keep up a resourceful attitude toward money and its potential.

And by all means be sure your present income continues to rise at least as much as the cost of living increases, preferably several percentage points more. Keep in mind the following examples that show that inflation is really not so bad as you may think:

- The same loaf of bread that cost $1.19 in 1982 as of the end of 1996 cost $2.19 but is available at a day-old bake shop for $1.09, marked down to $.59 on Tuesdays.
- I still can get five-cent photocopies on special for two cents each.
- I chat from coast to coast for over an hour for what it cost for 15 minutes during the 1960s.
- I paid hundreds of dollars *less* in income taxes last year than on about the same amount of income ten years ago.
- A family of four can rent a $.99 video and be entertained for $.25 each.
- A gallon of gasoline is comparable to its price of 15 years ago.
- A 32-cent stamp costs less in proportion to one's income now than a five-cent stamp did 30 years ago.
- Food prices have remained consistent: A ten-pound bag of potatoes is $1.49, a gallon of milk is under $2, ground beef is about $2.25 a pound, and fresh produce is still plenty affordable when in season.
- Though medical care has become outrageous, knowledge of preventive care and technological improvements have helped offset some of these costs.
- New cars are priced as high as houses were not long ago, but with better technology, breakdowns are less frequent, and cars last longer and are more fuel efficient.

Health care, housing, child care, college education, bank fees, and new car prices appear to have skyrocketed during the past 10 to 20 years. However, wages and benefits in most areas of the economy have also increased considerably. A salary of $36,000 a year is triple the cost of a $1,000-a-month house payment (figures common in 1995). An income of $10,800 a year was triple the cost of a $300-a-month house payment back in the 1960s (figures common then). With the exception of isolated geographic areas where housing costs have jumped far beyond the average, the ability to afford a home is *not* significantly more difficult, despite so much talk to the contrary. Though child care costs have become very high, in families in which both parents work, this cost is offset when up to three children are involved in most cases. As for college education, more investing strategies, loans, grants, and scholarships are available than ever.

In actual dollars, which is what counts in real terms of purchasing power, inflation is usually compensated for in surprisingly small percentage raises as cited here. For example, my household recently received a $16-a-month property tax increase, a $15-a-month child care increase, a $10-a-month car insurance increase, and about $15 a month of other miscellaneous increases. With employer raises of only $.50 an hour we comfortably exceeded all increases. With the extra money we have only improved our lifestyle. Understandably life is not always this smooth, but with careful management one can keep inflation in the nominal category.

For the person who just left the hospital after a six-week stay, bought an average-priced new car, or is covering the costs of a child or two attending an Ivy League school, he or she is going to feel justified in tearing out these pages and uttering words I prefer not to repeat here! But it is true that on the average an argument *against* the actual effect of inflation can be presented, and improvements and *deflation* in others can balance off the real cost in time and energy spent.

Sure it is easy for you to be shocked when you recall prices of various items being so much lower. I recall in amazement when my mother told me it cost $11 a day to be hospitalized when I was born, but such amazement was no less when she said the household income was under $5,000 a year. I believe the fear of inflation is quite real, yet inflation itself is not. People fear inflation because it appears that it could affect their ability to sustain their lifestyles and, understandably, it could, but this is very unlikely. As further chapters will explain, countless methods of coming out way ahead of inflation exist!

MONEY AND YOUR EMOTIONS

Like so much of what makes up our emotional states, personalities, and opinions, our feelings and reactions toward money often relate to childhood. Ask yourself how your parents dealt with money when you were young. Consider the following questions to determine the origins of your attitudes toward money:

- Did you see your family as poor, middle class, or rich?
- Did your parents often discuss money in negative or positive terms or hardly talk about it at all?
- Were they obsessed with saving for the future even though it appeared to you that the future had already come?
- Was one parent more of a saver while the other spent more?
- Was money openly discussed in your family or were family finances kept more secret?
- Was thrift and delayed gratification emphasized?
- Were you informed that the cost of living on your own would be prohibitive if you did not do well in school?
- How much did your parents earn and how would it compare with today's wages, taking inflation into account?
- Did your parents work so hard during your childhood that you wished they could have spent more time with you?
- What religious/spiritual values were you exposed to and how do they now affect your attitudes about accumulating wealth?
- Do you now see money representing success, power, high intelligence, freedom, better sex, increased opportunity, health, and longevity?
- Did your parents experience any major financial windfalls or setbacks?

Another part of one's money personality may be brought out when one engages in a partnership with another person. Often when one partner tends to be a spender, the other will withdraw into being a tightwad or resentfully resign to seeing the other bottom out their bank account, no matter how much they earn. Such emotional conflicts are common in other aspects of relationships as well. People frequently enter relationships without being at an extreme but become this way as a reaction to their partner.

Money is exchanged for our birth, medical care, food, housing, water, electricity, telephone, taxes to provide services, transportation, computers, furnishings, vacations, child care, gifts, education, insurance, charity, and more. Clearly, money is something we must have in today's society. How we deal with money is critical in terms of being able to receive the most enjoyment it can bring and being a respected citizen of the society. I doubt you want to end up like the following real cases.

- A 76-year-old woman who saved $700,000 and lives in a dilapidated home got caught taking the skins off the bananas in the supermarket to pay pennies less for them when they were weighed.
- A 36-year-old woman who constantly gripes about bills to pay but overpaid her insurance companies and the IRS more than $5,000 a year.
- A father who earns $150,000 a year can't believe he can afford a second child.
- A 30-year-old woman who compulsively works nearly 18 hours a day earning more than $75,000 a year, even brings her work home, saving every cent she can, at the expense of spending almost no time with her family.
- A 44-year-old man who was in debt when earning $10,000 a year was still in debt at $25,000 a year, and still is in debt at $75,000 a year.
- A multimillionaire investor who admitted that, "If there was one dollar left in the world, he would put his life on the line to get it." He was known to have bathed in money and near the end of his life had to be forcefully held down by two emergency medical technicians to be kept from swallowing dollar bills.

Of course, some of these cases are extreme, but we all have the potential to move in such directions. Much of the great challenge in dealing with one's finances is learning how to recognize rational and irrational behaviors. The rational is generally realistic and is beneficial to the individual, while the irrational is based on fears and often is detrimental.

All of us fall into various emotional money states to some extent. Some people are so desperate for money that they will kill for a $20 bill, while some of the very wealthy are bored with life, believing they have used money for everything it can buy. Unfortunately, neither extreme has realized that money alone is not the only nor the most important ingredient of a fulfilling life even though it's undeniably high on the list.

What does money mean to you? Does money give you power, freedom, independence, confidence, security, love, or happiness? Is your personal, home, and work life reasonably satisfying so that if you could get a healthier grasp on your finances you would reach a far higher level of contentment? Even if other areas of your life are not up to the standards you would like, significantly improving your finances may enhance them. When you make your next purchase, ask whether it keeps you emotionally dependent on more purchases. Evaluate whether you are doing it to be accepted by others or for a quick fix, if the other areas of your life are understimulated.

To get a grasp on your emotions as they relate to money ask yourself some key questions:

- What is my version of the American dream in practical terms?
- Can I make a habit of investigating possible alternatives to purchasing products off the shelf at regular prices?
- What is my motivation for spending money and how do I perceive the value of what I purchase?
- What is my money personality and its origins such as family excess or deprivation?
- Can I understand the relationship between money, time, and the expenditure of energy and realize that they make up life itself?
- What is "enough" to me in terms of material contentment?
- Can I realize that much of inflation is more perceived than real?
- What types of emotional satisfaction do I believe money can bring me?
- Can I muster up more self-discipline to not only set goals but also to achieve them?

Seriously consider these questions and write down your responses to reinforce your awareness of personal financial issues, how you view money, and where you wish to go with it. To get control of your financial life, you first must understand your attitude toward money and its role in your life.

CHAPTER 3

Working for Wages
AND Wealth

Finding work that is interesting, satisfying, pays well enough, offers good growth potential, and is secure is among the most challenging adventures in life. This is more true now than ever. It seems that there are ever more hoops and hurdles to jump over, around, and through and still no guarantees at the end of the obstacle course. The key to success is in knowing which of those hoops and hurdles *count*, which ones to ignore, and when to move in another direction entirely. For example, when I felt trapped in low-paying jobs, I looked for other alternatives. The more I succeed in wealth building and now writing, the less burdensome my job feels. Yes, I now believe that my wealth-building strategies and writing will at some point place my job into the *optional* category.

Wisdom on Wealth

Finding work that is interesting, satisfying, pays well enough, offers good growth potential, and is secure is among the most challenging adventures in life.

Your work may be boring and/or low paying. Do you feel trapped in such a situation because you need the money and feel insecure trying something else more desirable? I always recommend trying to earn a living, maybe only part-time at first, doing what you *enjoy.* Normally, what you find interesting goes along with what you are naturally talented at and can lead to satisfying employment. Doing what you like is more important than the pay. Of course I am not advocating quitting a well-paying job to pursue what you like, unless you have a cushion of savings to fall back on or an inordinate amount of self-confidence. But you might want to find an occupation or two you enjoy (it's always good to have a backup), and experiment with it part-time or after work. Working as a temporary is another great way to sample other work opportunities.

EMPLOYMENT ETHICS

Let's face it. The essential value of your employment is the paycheck. Numerous surveys have demonstrated that more than half of the working people would quit their work tomorrow if they did not need the money. Most workers put up with a lot more than rush-hour traffic twice a day to get their paychecks. How deeply do you care about your job other than doing it well enough to keep that income rolling in? How much precious time have you wasted pretending to look busy? How often have you made personal calls on the job largely to escape the monotony? I have known of employees who will read paperback books in the rest room for a half hour while the boss is out, simply to kill time because they ran out of work to do. How often have you been treated worse by your employer than you might treat a fat cockroach crawling across your kitchen counter? I could nearly write another book about the abuse of authority by employers. Robert Hochheiser, in his book, *How to Work for a Jerk* (Vintage Books), makes an entertaining attempt at this. Or are you among the fortunate who really enjoy and feel productive in your work, and like your boss and coworkers? There are plenty who neither love nor hate their work, but who find the routine provides a needed structure to their lives.

Can you cope with your employment? The answer needs to be *yes,* if your only alternative is *unemployment.* Your work priorities should be to please your employer (though not at the cost of making yourself miserable), to maintain a positive attitude, to avoid highly personal/controversial interactions with fellow employees, to dress professionally, to be open to learning new skills that can make you more indispensable, to get the most mileage from your paycheck, and to seek opportunities for more fulfilling and better-paying work.

Let's carefully weigh and balance what more pay and receiving a promotion really means to your satisfaction. Do you like your "meaningless, repetitious" job despite the low pay because you prefer not to deal with the greater responsibilities and stress that come with "moving up the ladder"? Perhaps you prefer to save your mental energy for projects and interests outside of the workplace, or you don't care for the longer hours required from a better-paying position. If all this is true, but you are still accepting a promotion because you think you need the higher salary, think again. By applying the principles of resourcefulness discussed in later chapters, you will realize that your present income is not so much the issue as is the income you think you need to sustain your lifestyle.

What about those who prefer ever greater challenges on the job and prefer to wind down and engage in more recreational activities beyond the workplace? For those who have the appropriate personality and really enjoy the added stress, responsibilities, and time, go and devote yourselves fully to the corporation! The bottom line is to arrange your life around what you *enjoy*, and leave slavery to the dollar behind you, as soon as possible. After reading this book I expect that you soon will be able to turn things around and let dollars do more of the work for you.

THE COST OF WORKING

Employment outside the home involves several expenses that can impact your take-home pay. They consist of transportation, which means all the costs involved in maintaining a car or the cost of using public transportation, work clothing and its maintenance, lunches out with employees, holiday and birthday gifts, potluck meals, and various requests for donations.

You give a lot of your *time* as necessitated by your job that you are *not compensated* for. You wash, shave or make yourself up, and dress to a far greater degree than if you did not have to go to work. You may bag your lunch or spend money buying lunch, which consumes time and/or money you would not have to spend if you stay home. And you may spend one to two hours a day with your right foot on the gas pedal or trust another driver, which adds greater risk to your life. All of this time may not have a direct cost in dollars, but it sure adds up in lost personal time to be with your friends or family, pursue your hobbies, start a business, read, write, watch TV, play tennis, call someone, and travel. When you also account for unpaid work you may have to bring home, the value your paid wage may be cut by 20 to 40 percent. Take into account child care costs and the tax differential if you have a high-paid spouse, and your actual pay could drop up to 80 percent. With the advancement of technology, several million people already telecommute and hopefully many more will follow, greatly increasing the efficiency for employees and employers.

GETTING DECENT RAISES

When it comes to work and pay, the name of the game is to receive as much compensation as is reasonable, and to ensure more and better raises in the future. Many employers provide cost-of-living adjustments once every year or two, but merit raises depend more on you. In addition to providing satisfying contributions to your employer, being highly efficient with your time and going beyond the call of duty to cooperate and occasionally working a modest amount of unpaid overtime willingly may help. There is a fine line, however, between extending yourself occasionally and being exploited.

To move up, get yourself the skills you need to make yourself irreplaceable, assuming you wish to stay with this employer for a long time. If your boss will train you, be a sponge! Take night courses if they will provide you with the needed skills or invest in or borrow the equipment you need to become proficient. Become broad-based in your abilities at work. Attendance and punctuality are critical factors among many employers in their employee evaluations as well. Being on time and taking proper breaks should be the easiest way to please an employer. You must learn the personality types of your supervisor and managers and find out what they respond to positively.

Wisdom on Wealth

An important message I wish to communicate throughout this book is that *small amounts matter*.

So what can even a small raise mean to you? A lot! Just getting 25 cents more per hour is $10 a week or $520 a year. Just this small raise more than offsets all my cost-of-living increases in 1996. And, of course 50 cents an hour is $1,040 a year, while a dollar an hour is $2,080 annually. My recommendation for raises is to figure out your monthly cost-of-living increase compared with the past year or the last time you received a raise, take the portion needed from the raise to compensate for the increased cost of living, take another portion to boost your lifestyle, and another portion to begin or increase your saving and investing. Should you experience a spike in your cost of living that is beyond your control and exceptionally high, consider not boosting your lifestyle temporarily and/or seek out some of the alternative income strategies for extra income discussed in this book. Because of the compounding effect, the more frequently you receive a raise, the faster you can reach your goals.

BENEFITS

Many employers provide varying combinations of benefits such as health insurance, life insurance, tax-deferred retirement savings plans and pensions, profit sharing, credit union membership, paid sick and vacation time, sabbatical leaves, parental leaves, maternity pay, on-site child care, severance pay, and more. Virtually no employer provides *all* of these, for doing so probably would be prohibitive in cost. In many cases, employees must share in the costs of some benefits. From a financial standpoint, the health insurance and retirement plans and pensions are likely to be the most valuable to employees. Some employers provide health coverage free of cost to employees, though it can cost a fortune to insure a spouse and dependent family members. Most require an employee contribution. Some employers offer what is called a flexible spending account that is money taken from your paycheck before taxes to cover the cost of certain benefits such as life, health, disability insurance, and child care. This can work to your benefit only if you really want or need all these benefits. For example, if your spouse has you and your children covered for health insurance at a good rate under his or her employer plan, you may emphasize more life and disability coverage from your employer. But budget carefully, because funds placed into such an account revert back to the employer by the end of the year if they are not spent. And don't forget to keep up-to-date on how much sick, vacation, and personal leave time you have accumulated, under what conditions to exercise it, and the time frame in which it must be used.

A variety of pension and retirement account plans are available. Some employers have guaranteed benefit plans that provide annuitized payments for life after an employee is "vested," which usually requires a minimum of five years of employment with a company. Of course, benefits increase with one's length of employment beyond the vesting requirement. Also existing are such excellent plans as the 401(k), 403(b), Simplified Employee Pension (SEP), and Keogh, some of which are based on employee contributions that the employer matches, up to certain limits. For example, an employer might contribute 50 percent or more of its own funds, subject to dollar limits to match your untaxed contribution out of your paycheck until you withdraw it many years later at retirement. This means that you are making a whopping 50 percent return on your money every year—better than any investment can even approach! You also may have choices of how to invest these funds to increase your return even more. Some employers offer discount stock options, or the opportunity to buy company stock below present value, to place in retirement plans. This can be a good opportunity, though the stocks should be researched before making a strong commitment. Because retirement funds are tax-deferred, you can add even more to your rate of return. If your employer offers tax-deferred savings/retirement plans, take full advantage of them, for it is possible to accumulate hundreds of thousands of dollars in them over the years. For more information on investing, see Chapter 11.

Wisdom on Wealth

If your employer offers tax-deferred savings/ retirement plans, take full advantage of them, for it is possible to accumulate hundreds of thousands of dollars in them over the years.

TERMINATION

Depending on the circumstances under which you depart from your employer, you may be eligible to collect unemployment benefits for a period of time, normally 26 weeks. The amount of weekly benefits are based on recent wages and other current employer benefits and government entitlements. Keep in mind that voluntarily quitting usually bars you from collecting unemployment insurance, so have plans to keep income coming in if you make this choice. For information check with your state employment office.

SELF-EMPLOYMENT

Many people have the dream of being self-employed. They figure they will be able to leave the "rat race" of long commutes, time clocks, high pressure, disputes with employers, and the confinement of low income with little potential for upward mobility. They hope for freedom to set their own hours, be their own boss, have more opportunities to be creative, and earn more money. For some, self-employment is a dream come true, but not for all. In addition to downsizing and major technological innovations that have cost countless employees their jobs, many people now are choosing to make changes within their field or start entirely new careers. The bottom line for everyone today is to experience fulfillment from work whether self-employed or not.

If you have determined that you are cut out for self-employment, how can being self-employed increase your wealth at least as much as working for someone else?

- You are not at the mercy of a company whose motive is cost-containment that limits your wage and must follow laws that can place further restrictions on your earning potential.
- When you own your own company you have more freedom to pay yourself more, work as many hours as you want, and invest profits as you see fit.
- Becoming self-employed is normally based on the assumption that you have a skill you like and are good at, therefore, increasing your satisfaction in life.
- Operating a business is one of the best ways to learn about how money works, for doing so may force on you a healthy sense of financial discipline.

When you are self-employed, you are in business for yourself. A whole new set of rules applies, such as paying estimated taxes, managing a business bank account that operates differently from a personal one (not to your advantage), perhaps managing employees and employee benefits, and a legal responsibility to your customers. Products and/or services must be priced and packaged properly and delivered in a timely manner. Refunds or credits may have to be offered. Inventory that will not sell at any price will have to be stored or discarded at a loss. You will have to decide whether to incorporate, be a sole proprietorship, or assume some other business classification. When a machine breaks down, the roof leaks, or the rent goes up, full responsibility may fall on your back. An accounting system will have to be set up to keep records of all the incoming and outgoing funds, and taxes are certain to be more complex.

In some cases self-employment is *more stressful* than putting in your eight hours for a predictable sum of money and arriving home with *few, if any*, thoughts about work. The self-employed person always has some work responsibilities hanging in the wind. But if he or she enjoys what he or she does, this is fine. The exciting aspect of self-employment is that what you put in is what you receive, unlike when you are employed by someone else. You can put in *your* creativity, intelligence, time, and energy rather than being restricted by a superior who may not support many of your good hunches. According to Standard & Poors, more than 22 million people are self-employed and about 4 million businesses are started each year.

What can you do to earn a good living being self-employed? To figure this out you will have to write down the things you enjoy that also have the potential to generate income. Then research what level of commitment it takes to enjoy a high chance of success in your areas of interest. Determine your initial investment of money and time. Do you have the natural talents to develop employment from your home? Millions of people are well employed at home with little more than a telephone and a computer. Free-lance art, photography, and writing lend themselves well to a home-based business. Software and financial consultants may work from home as well.

A potentially large risk is involved in becoming self-employed. Unless you have a lot of cash to draw from, which is not needed for basic living expenses, and you can afford to quit your job, it is best to phase in self-employment gradually. Another possibility is to use extended time off, such as teachers get in the summer, to start a business. If it appears by the end of the summer that the business has reasonable potential to succeed, you can calculate if it is worth giving up teaching, working part-time, or hiring someone to keep the business operating, even if temporarily running at a loss. Perhaps you have a close relative who is retired and is willing to volunteer some time to run the business or provide certain other needed service in your home such as child care, cleaning, or cooking to give you time to work at the business. If that person believes in what you are doing and is able to assist you financially, you might receive a modest loan of some cash to hold things over. These early stages of starting a business are the toughest on your emotions and pocketbook, too. If this business is really a dream for you and your expectations are realistic, however, it may be worth the hard work and risks for a period of time. Certainly, at some point you will have to decide to what extent you want to continue investing time, energy, and money into a new business or whether to cut your losses if things are not improving. Only you can determine this.

Many ways exist in which the self-employed person can save money, whether the business is small or large. Here are a few major ways:

- Seek out free or low-cost publicity that can translate into advertising. For example, get featured in newspapers and magazines, be interviewed on television and radio talk shows or news spots, get a write-up in your college alumni and employer bulletins, and check out the potential of the Internet.
- Don't rush too fast into buying an array of computers, office furniture, copiers, high-priced advertising, and a state-of-the-art telephone system. Early in the life of a small business is when things are the most vulnerable. Be frugal but know when a capital investment pays off.
- Do your own market research using local resources and the Internet to get virtually free information.
- Offer free product demonstrations and give away samples.
- Research the lowest-cost method of borrowing money.
- Research the lowest-cost space rental, implement utility cost-reduction strategies, and learn where to purchase materials at rock-bottom prices.
- Be a firm negotiator and use credit to your advantage.
- Don't spend money because you can write it off on your taxes. Funds not spent will benefit you more than money spent minus a tax deduction.

Almost immediately, when others hear that you are now "in business for yourself," you may be viewed differently. Most will respect you, but some will water down what you are doing and arouse your fears that you are taking too high a risk, might fail, and may say you should not have left the security of that stable paycheck. Some will think you now are wealthy because you were able to take such a risk and leave the predictable paycheck behind. A reasonable sum of cash generally is often required to start a business, but by no means does the decision to become self-employed mean that you are *wealthy*. In fact, quite the opposite often is the case, for start-up costs can be very high and many months or even a year or two may pass before a profit is established. Living off savings or a spouse's salary during this interim period may be a necessity, in addition to having to borrow funds.

Wisdom on Wealth

Funds not spent will benefit you more than money spent minus a tax deduction.

INCOME ALTERNATIVES

Other than engaging in illegal activities or at least unethical ones, how else can you receive supplemental income besides working more hours in the traditional sense? One way is through investing, which is covered in Chapter 11. Investing is a great goal to aim for, but it is generally more long-term and chances are you would like more *present* income.

There are dozens of ways to bring in more income. Here are just a few:

- Comic book collectors trade in comics and bring in several extra thousand dollars a year. The same can apply to a variety of collectibles, from stamps and coins to antique furniture and sports cards.
- If you have the inclination, it is possible to get great deals on used cars, fix and clean them up, and sell them at a premium.
- I met a man who flies around the country buying antique cameras, resells them from his home and by mail order, and claims

that he grossed more than $70,000 a year and netted close to $30,000.

- How about doing some bartering? If scheduling can be arranged, exchanging child care can work out well.
- Perhaps you can rent a room in your home to a responsible college student or have this person accomplish certain chores that you may not wish to do.
- Do you have any elderly or handicapped people in your neighborhood? They may need some part-time services such as grocery buying, yard care, or house cleaning.
- Checking the employment classifieds in your newspaper, you may find part-time telemarketing, survey, or appointment setting telephone work, which can be performed from your home telephone.
- What about recycling? I recall working for a company in which employees were permitted to occasionally load up their personal vehicles with aluminum printing plates, trashed office paper, and soda cans. They then drove to the recycling center and walked away with $50 to $100.
- Do you have several neighbors who need a particular service that requires the use of power equipment they don't own? For example, you could rent a high-pressured water power machine for $60 and power-clean your driveway and house and then charge five neighbors $20 to $25 each to clean theirs.
- I once charged nine students only $20 each to drive them round-trip from Boston to Washington, D.C., in my van, which after gas and tolls, cost me about $80. This was truly a win-win situation!
- Consider participating in medical and pharmaceutical studies. I have seen advertisements in my newspaper for such studies and participated in some. They pay from as little as $75 up to more than $4,000. Of course, the more they pay, the heavier the commitment can be, such as sleeping in a laboratory's dorm over the course of several weekends. Because I have always wondered what causes me to occasionally sneeze 150+ times in a couple of hours, while other times months can pass without so much as an itchy nose, I participated in a medical study. My out-of-pocket costs for an allergy evaluation could have been nearly $1,000, but I received a battery of testing, free EKG, free medication, and was paid $400. How about that? *Making* money off of health care instead of *spending* it!

- Donate blood plasma. Doing so can pay $20 to $25 per donation for about an hour and a half, can be done twice a week, has no health risks, and assists in saving the lives of others.
- Prepare and hand out food samples in grocery stores. While this may sound easy and fun, the times I have scooped 1,200 ice-cream cones or stabbed 2,600 strawberries into shortcake in one shift has been exhausting to say the least! Food demonstrations pay $50 to 75 for an eight-hour shift.
- Being an extra in a movie production is another employment opportunity if you are fortunate enough to have movies made in your town. Contact your local film guild to check out this possibility. Doing so should pay from $50 to $150 per shift, depending on circumstances.

There is always a way to make money. In these days of reportedly less income security, part-time work, alternative income sources, and investing are flourishing.

Wisdom on Wealth

Just remember it's as important to find something that you enjoy doing as it is something that you are good at. Once you find your niche, financial independence and success will be well within your grasp.

CHAPTER 4

Achieving Wealth as a Family

Just what makes money such a sensitive area in our lives to deal with? Well, it's not difficult to understand. With our attachments to money being so strong, conscious or not, it is no wonder that having to share our earning, spending, saving, and investing habits with others is not always going to be clear sailing.

Everyone views money differently, but certain major characteristics identify money behaviors among people. Look at the money behavior chart on page 39 and ask yourself which category you belong in.

Everyone has some combination of these tendencies, to greater or lesser degrees. *Balance* is the key.

There are good reasons why money arguments are the number one cause of divorce. Even couples who come from the same background with similar money styles may disagree. Most people have not operated their own businesses nor had to share financial decisions before being married. Though many singles find money frustrating to deal with, *they alone* are in control of it. Come on! Let's face it. We are all self-centered at heart. We spend our time and energy working hard to get money and therefore want to decide the fate of it. We are not born wanting to share, especially in the decision-making processes involving how resources are utilized.

Money Behavior Chart	
Present-Focused	Financial priorities tend to focus on present needs of home and family
Future-Focused	Tends to push for higher and financial goals
Freewheelers	Cash large chunks of their paychecks and spend the money as they see fit
Compulsive Spenders	Spend money to temporarily raise their self-esteem
Gamblers	Have unrealistic grandiose dreams and routinely take high risks
Security-Conscious	Always choose the least risky path to financial security
Philanthropist	Constantly donating money to charities
Miser	Extreme savers, worship money daily

A marriage is a lot more than a love relationship. It is a *business partnership* as well, as any married person can testify. Whether one or both partners earn money, the door is wide open for disagreements over how limited incoming and outgoing resources are to be dealt with: Should we remodel the bathroom or contribute to our IRAs? Does our four-year-old need a pair of $40 shoes that she will outgrow in six months or will the $8 pair at Wal-Mart do? Or should we get the ones from the garage sale for $1? How can we spend less on Christmas this year without the in-laws thinking we are "selfish tightwads"? Can't you ever treat yourself now instead of thinking about the future? The future is already here! Sound familiar? A list of this sort could go on for pages.

Attitudes about money start in childhood through observing how our parents dealt with their finances. Did your parents argue a lot about how money should be spent or regularly show frustration at the high costs of living? Was one of them a tightwad and the other a spender? Coming to an understanding of what models we had growing up can create empathy toward each other and begin the process of reducing marital stress.

> ## Wisdom on Wealth
>
> A marriage is a lot more than a love relationship. It is a *business partnership* as well, as any married person can testify.

Each person brings to a marriage his or her individual style, attitudes, and values about money. What is your money style? Are you the spender or the saver? Do you consider yourself to be more present- or future-focused when you think of financial security? Take a look at the money behavior chart on page 39. Think about your money style and your spouse's, too. You see, for better or worse, savers and spenders tend to marry one another. The result is often conflicting attitudes and values on money and how it should be spent and invested. Long before the champagne reception, set time aside to discuss money matters. Here are some questions to launch you in the right direction to financial harmony.

- Can you define your spouse's attitudes and values about money?
- Do your spending styles match or clash?
- Should you be accountable to each other for all your spending or should you each have a sense of privacy?
- What are your savings goals (vacation, new car, down payment on a home, starting a family, or early retirement)?
- Is there going to be a significant decrease in household income if you or your spouse should decide to return to college or have a child?
- What are each of you bringing in terms of assets to the marriage, such as stocks, property, debts, and family obligations?
- Does one of you tend to spend more in the present while the other emphasizes securing the future?
- How do your childhood and family money values differ? Who is more goal-oriented?
- In what areas are your financial dreams different? Include both short- and long-term goals.

Once you have carefully discussed and come to terms with this list, date and sign it. Treating such matters in a factual and practical fashion will allow you to develop a sense of honesty, fairness, and trust in your marriage. After all, marriage is an economic contract between two caring people that has legal obligations, responsibilities, and consequences.

TEN STEPS TO HANDLING HOUSEHOLD MONEY

In addition to methods of keeping financial conflict at bay, several ways of improving efficiency in a household's cash flow are available. Here are some important ones:

1. Find out if your management or mortgage company, telephone company, utility, or any other place you make regular payments to will make *automatic drafts* from your bank account. This service is usually free, and saves you the effort of writing checks, stamping envelopes, and mailing payments. The businesses you deal with on this basis will indicate to you in advance how much bills will be, normally giving you plenty of time to ensure that enough funds are available in the account. All you have to do is subtract the money as if you wrote a check.
2. Pay by telephone or make payments from your computer. It is generally only worth spending the money on the software and $10 to $20 monthly fees if you have a lot of separate bills to pay each month.
3. Pay several months' worth of bills *all at once*. In addition to saving time and the postage needed to pay these bills each month, some companies may give you a discount for paying ahead of time. In some cases, a free month's service is provided by the company to receive your investable funds far in advance. Most utility, cable TV, and telephone companies accept prepayments.
4. Depending on your money personality and if in a joint relationship, you may find it beneficial to have one joint checking account, separate accounts, or two separate accounts and one joint account to pay strictly joint essential bills such as housing, utilities, and food.
5. Based on your personal preference, you may discover that it simplifies your finances to withdraw from your bank an estimated lump of *cash* at the beginning of each month to cover such expenses as food, gasoline, minor hardware, auto parts, cosmetics, tithing, and other miscellaneous things. Doing so reduces the number of checks to account for, significantly reducing efforts in checkbook balancing.
6. Another option is to pay for practically everything on just *one credit card* which can all be covered through writing just *one check* a month.

7. If using a computer saves time and makes household budgeting more convenient, look into obtaining software for this purpose.
8. Check out the Internet for more shopping opportunities. Doing so saves gas, car use, time, and money, and has become very secure.
9. Avoid family financial conflicts by holding money meetings at least once a month and being open-minded in terms of the potential and flexibility of money. Establish a few financial responsibility rules.
10. Be honest with other adults who share the household finances with you. Secretly saving or spending will catch up with you, and when it does this will be no party!

INSTILLING HEALTHY MONEY VALUES

I thought it was sad when a neighbor admitted to my wife that her four-year-old told her, "Mommy, I don't want a boat. I want more time with you." He had heard the mother mention that she and her husband were each working two full-time jobs around the clock to save up for a new boat. Clearly a portion of our society places a higher value on material objects rather than on other human beings. This diminished socialization crosses over into adult friendships as well, with adults also having less time for each other. No doubt this is one reason for renewed interest in various forms of spirituality.

Because of the pressures people place on themselves to acquire material wealth, there is a segment of poorly nurtured children in our culture. They have tendencies toward negative directions as they grow, higher stressed mothers and fathers to deal with, less healthy spontaneous social activity, and higher levels of anxiety over competing to get into "the best" college and find a good job. With more efficient money and time budgeting, most of these pressures can be relaxed.

As children grow, it is essential that you instill healthy money values in them. Many people recall opening their first passbook savings account during grade school with a dollar or two, first adding 25 cents a week, then 50, and finally watching it grow to more than $10 over a number of months. I remember saving for a couple of months to get $3 to buy something for my hobbies.

Wisdom on Wealth

As children grow, it is essential that you instill healthy money values in them.

By the age of three, many children already understand that one must have money to receive various items or services in return. They realize that the merry-go-round or gum-ball machine requires a coin. Parents can let them place the coin in the machine and let them hand the cash to the cashier in the grocery store. By the age of five, children have a clear grasp of money's value, at a time when more and more teaching opportunities arise.

THE ALLOWANCE

Children normally are mature enough to handle receiving a small allowance by the age of six or seven. It is most effective to pay it to them on a consistent basis, such as every Thursday morning. The main purpose of an allowance is for children to learn to make choices within economic limitations. Initially, young children need to have the freedom to spend small change as they wish, to obtain a feel for what money can buy. Gradually they can be encouraged to set financial goals, such as saving up for a football or a computer game. And there is a health aspect regarding how money is spent, which parents may have to communicate. It's fine to let children see that if they buy candy and soft drinks each week, the football purchase will be delayed. But when costly dental fillings result from unhealthy habits, this kind of spending will have to be curtailed. I also see nothing wrong with demonstrating that the $1.50 spent on such items accumulates to $15 after ten weeks, $30 after 20 weeks, etc.

After a child has received an allowance for a year or so, a light amount of forced saving may be in order, with a certain portion of each payment going into the bank. Starting a savings plan when young encourages children to continue this behavior into childhood. Keep in mind that depending on the age of your child and the type of interest he or she has in money, the child may desire to save a considerable amount of his or her allowance in the bank for more lasting purchases or even more distant goals. According to B. Douglas Bernheim, an economist at Stanford University, in the summer/fall *Kemper Reports*, there are strong connections between childhood money experiences and adult behavior. He claims that children who received allowances saved, on average, 36 percent more as adults, and that those who maintained bank accounts as children saved 108 percent more for their retirement during adulthood.

With some searching, banks can be found that still will accept low-balance accounts for children or a parent can deposit a minimum amount in his or her account that will permanently be subtracted from the balance. In other words, if your bank requires a savings account with a $250 minimum, deposit the minimum in your name. Any amount over the minimum then will belong to your child. Of course, one day in the future you may let the minimum become your child's money. If parents take an active interest in their children's saving and spending habits, they can help keep their children from being too extreme either as misers or spenders. There are no guarantees, however, of how the children will turn out as adults—no matter what Freud said about potty training time being a factor in forecasting future money behaviors! Having children involved in simple matters such as clipping coupons, balancing a checkbook, viewing the mortgage statement, or assisting with tax forms is great experience. By adolescence it is good to encourage them to occasionally read the business pages in the newspaper or magazines or watch economic information on television to get a feel for what is going on in the economic world.

Once children reach the age of eight to ten years, most love to receive bank statements in the mail and find it interesting to watch their balance grow from interest or dividends. Gradually you can discuss in more detail how to save some money in the account, spend some on *needs* such as clothing and school supplies, and spend some more on *wants* such as games, expensive sneakers, or eating out.

As children grow and can perform more complex house and garden work, you may consider supplementing their allowance for significant jobs that are well beyond the weekly routine of cleaning the bathroom, vacuuming, dusting, and mowing the lawn. Such work includes washing cars, cleaning the gutters, washing windows, cleaning out the garage, or major yard work. Children like to work for money as they mature, rather than receive cash arbitrarily because it's Wednesday evening or Saturday morning. Saturday morning is not recommended as a good time to give allowances because children are more likely to spend money spontaneously on weekends. Reaffirming that it takes work to get money can't hurt, either.

GIVING CHILDREN MONEY CONFIDENCE

Another area parents simply can't ignore is the effect of peer pressure on children, especially teens. Though many of us grew out of this stage years ago, we need to be understanding because this behavior is normal for children, to an extent. There will always be a child or several children who possess certain types of clothes, bicycles, sporting equipment, hair styles, cars, etc., which create envy in others. In some parts of the country children have murdered each other to get a specific style of jacket. Children are constantly poking fun at each other over what they are wearing. It takes a lot of self-confidence and a powerful sense of individuality in children to simply shrug off such comments from others. The children who are happy and proud of themselves and their family values, although not overly so, will be the most likely to ignore the pressure and enjoy being themselves. If they have a clear understanding of why their winter jackets came from a consignment store instead of the mall, such healthy levels of confidence may be the norm.

Wisdom on Wealth

Children make psychological connections between money and love, money and approval or disapproval, money and good school performance, money and obedience, and even money as a way to express annoyance.

It is not rare for parents to say to their 15-year-old, "Here's $20. Go have some fun"—as if the only way to enjoy oneself is to spend. Acting in such a manner not only communicates to the child that pleasure must involve spending, but that the parents are trying to get him or her out of the house. As for parents using money as a means to discipline or motivate a child to achieve, I find this practice questionable because it emphasizes money even more to young people.

Early on, boys and girls learn to associate social and moral values with a given economic reality. Miserly, frugal parents value money differently than laid-back spenders. Fortunately, many are somewhere in the middle.

Certain parents doing quite well for themselves often recall their own hard struggles back in their 20s and 30s and vow to give their children "everything." Other parents are downright wealthy, yet place strict demands on their children, encourage thrift, and even deny what they have beyond what the eye can see. And there are parents who are unable to spend money on themselves but will provide nearly anything for their children. I believe that both parents and children should respect the significance of money, enjoy it, yet not be obsessed by it. This is not always an easy balance to maintain. To boost a young adult's financial confidence, try the following:

- Involve adolescents in everyday, practical financial responsibilities such as income taxes, mortgage and utility payments, and checkbook balancing.
- Demonstrate the rewards of delayed gratification through modeling, for example, paying in cash instead of charging.
- Convey the pleasurable aspects of money more than the negative ones and avoid money arguments around all children.
- Teach the relative value of money through examples such as comparing prices in stores and costs of activities, services, and products—getting the message across that pleasure doesn't always have to be measured in dollars.
- As a living example, communicate a simple, balanced sense of thriftiness, economy, and resourcefulness while living a fulfilling life. Not everything has to be purchased at a garage sale or a secondhand shop, nor does the mall have to be your main shopping source.

When children are in the right mood, the following statements can be analyzed with young people over the age of 12. Conversation of this type can enlighten parents about their children's money attitudes as well as further educate the children.

- The best things in life are free.
- Anything worth doing is worth doing well.
- Consumers buy what they like best.
- People would be better off if they just had more money.
- Good consumers seek all the information they can about a product before they buy it.
- Life is priceless.
- People who work hard get the highest wages.
- The more useful a product, the more it costs.

THE WORKING TEEN

By the age of 14, teenagers may legally hold down jobs, although only on a part-time basis during the school year. Surveys show that most teens want to work and prefer to obtain money by working than from their mom and dad. Some jobs offer teens good work experience, but most are entry-level service occupations involving repetitious acts that may be boring, require late evening hours, offer poor working conditions, and merely provide employees with small paychecks. It is common for teens to earn about $300 to $1,000 a month. Most live very much in the present, which is healthy and expected behavior for this age. Adolescents now spend more than $52 billion a year, primarily on themselves. As they begin working, they need to be encouraged to save something extra, whether it be for a car, college, or hard times finding work later. Depending on the extent to which parents continue to pay for clothing, haircuts, dental bills, assistance in buying a car (I recommend delaying car purchases as long as possible), etc., they can negotiate how much of their teen's earnings must be saved for college or other future expenses. Once working teens understand the concept of loans, they can be introduced to the world of credit. You can charge them interest like a credit card would. Once they handle this process well, young adults can be encouraged to apply for a real credit card.

There is hope for teens to find work other than flipping burgers. It may take more creativity and networking from parents and children, but the results will be worth the effort. Newspaper delivery and modeling are the only two areas of employment permitted by law for children under the age of 14 to perform on a regular basis. But many are mature enough to baby-sit, do lawn and garden work, pet care, window cleaning, and painting. Such work can be performed on a casual basis legally; in fact, a 9-year-old might wash the neighbor's car better than a 17-year-old, who expects a greater challenge.

For older adolescents plenty of alternative job opportunities are available. Here are a few suggestions:

- Working for a family business. A friend of mine serviced and sold bicycles out of his cellar successfully all through high school.
- For under $15, one can buy the supplies to clean VCRs and then charge $30 a cleaning.
- Painting address numbers on curbs requires little more than a few stencils and the paint.
- Cleaning gutters needs little more than a pair of work gloves and a ladder, which already may be in your garage. Keep in mind that

gutter cleaning can run some safety and liability risks. No amount of money is worth falling from the second-story roof!
- House painting is always in demand.
- Be a day-camp counselor.
- The growing elderly population needs food prepared and delivered along with a host of other personal-care services.
- House cleaning pays surprisingly well.
- Food demonstrations in grocery stores pay $7 to $8 per hour and require only a card table, tablecloth, plastic food-handling gloves, cooking skillet, and basic utensils. This is good experience working with the public.
- Perhaps your teens are bilingual enough to assist others with translating or learning English, even if they don't know their language well.
- They can tutor younger children in whatever subject they are comfortable with.
- What about arts and crafts? Teens can sew, bake and decorate cakes, create signs, do paste-up work, or make other crafts that can be sold at Christmas bazaars and art shows. When selling my color photographs, I learned more and loved what I was doing more than any other occupation I have had to date!
- If your children can write, they can contribute articles or poetry to local newspapers and magazines.
- Maybe they can conduct telephone surveys, use a personal computer for profit, repair old books, deliver telephone books, paint portraits, read to the blind, or buy items at garage sales and then recondition and resell them out of your garage.
- They might be able to act as a contractor's assistant—after taking proper safety precautions. If your child is so inclined and interested, this could turn into an apprenticeship.
- They may be skilled enough to enter contests in art, music, spelling, or writing, for example, that can lead to awards such as scholarships to college or trips abroad.

TEACHING ACCOUNTABILITY AND RESPONSIBILITY

Because money brings about the instant gratification so important to teens, they sometimes let work conflict with their studies. When this happens, parents must set limits and make it clear that work hours will have to be curtailed until grades rise again. It may be more prudent to already have such limits as a preventive measure. Marks on a report card don't provide the quick lift of a full wallet for most teens. Similarly, an A or B grade doesn't buy a beautiful dress or favorite compact disks. The most unfortunate occurrence in some families is when parents discover that their teen's earnings are supporting a drug, smoking, or alcohol habit. And, worse yet, evidence shows that if this is the case, shutting off the cash flow is not necessarily the most effective method of intervention.

Parents must account for their teen's earnings and spending. Once children have earned income, be sure to assist them in opening an individual retirement account. Talking to 15-year-olds about saving until 65 is not recommended, other than to briefly open their minds to the concept of long-term, tax-deferred accumulation. Although college and a car may seem to be a higher priority at the time, placing a few hundred dollars a year into an IRA will pay off handsomely many years later, because of getting an earlier start on compounding. Realizing the rewards of effortless earning is a critical step in financial maturity. After all, is there anyone who would turn down the offer of being able to earn money while playing golf or watching a favorite film instead of being at the office? Help your child plant his or her own money tree that can bear fruit indefinitely, once it matures.

Wisdom on Wealth

Most children are happier when they are provided with new freedoms, privileges, and approval for help with house chores than just being handed cash.

Be honest with your children about the cost of living by showing them your monthly bills and what makes some bills higher one month than another. As your children become young adults, you may show them your paycheck stub so they will have a full grasp of incoming and outgoing funds.

Also, make it clear that *choices* exist in what sort of lifestyle to choose. Encourage good buying habits and appropriate telephone use, help your child set up a checking account and fill out tax forms together, demonstrate the wise use of energy and water, preventive health, and the variety of housing options. Explain how to establish credit. These topics can be brought up and explored as an adolescent child shows interest. These topics need to be discussed with positive enthusiasm—not high pressure.

If your children should demonstrate genuine curiosity about more sophisticated places to put money than the local bank, then by all means, teach them all they want to know! You can communicate the message that accumulation and sound money management are roads to prosperity, independence, and a comfortable lifestyle. Some children show serious interest in the stock market as young as the age of eight, including a few who have amassed several thousands of dollars by the age of ten!

Whenever they are interested and certainly by their teen years, children must be introduced to the costs of living. You can share classified advertisements in newspapers that show the costs of buying or renting housing along with the employment section. Also, be sure to instill the concepts of buying over time and the enormous cost of interest in the purchase of a house with a mortgage. An amortization chart shows this very clearly. Compare mortgage and other expenses associated with ownership to renting. Have your children understand all the costs of owning their own cars and the options for receiving medical care affordably as well as reviewing various types of insurance. And in addition to a college fund you have set up from early on, during adolescence have your children save significant portions of their earnings for college goals. Students who have worked hard to pay for much of college tend to take the work more seriously and perform better, while young people who are undecided in career choices may end up partying away the first couple of semesters.

For those who are parents, planning to become parents, or work in some positions as educators, this information should give you the foundation for training children on how to handle money. Many people enter adulthood with so little understanding of money. Unless our parents were financial planners or active investors, chances are that we learned little more than how to spend the money we earn to maintain our basic needs and increase our pleasure. Instilling responsible financial behavior early on in a child's life can mean the difference between an adult who is constantly worried about money and one who enjoys a balanced and productive life.

Having all family members well informed on basic family finance, from 10-year-old grandchildren to 90-year-old grandparents, can only lead to continued family prosperity for generations to come. Just establishing a family tradition of saving at least 10 percent of wages and investing it versus the family who lives on the edge could increase a typical family's wealth over generations by more than a million dollars. Do the grandchildren have some concept of the rewards of delayed gratification? Have their parents reaped the rewards of not merely disciplined saving through their employers, but acquired the money savvy to enjoy the satisfaction of living while spending less than their neighbors? Has the grandparent rewarded himself or herself with what money can buy and engaged in appropriate death-planning and wealth-preservation strategies? Being alert to one's family finances and staying disciplined while remaining balanced will keep up a high level of wealth and health.

CHAPTER 5

Letting Credit Work
FOR You

Credit is a valuable financial resource to draw from for everyone and frequently a major factor in the creation of dreams. Credit adds another dimension to the value of money, in a sense multiplying its value. Here are the major reasons why credit may benefit you:

- To have immediate access to money almost anywhere, anytime.
- To demonstrate financial responsibility. In addition to lending institutions, prospective employers and auto insurance companies commonly do credit checks when considering to hire and insure.
- To qualify for a home mortgage, car loan, college loan, credit cards, rental leases, rental cars, and more.
- To start businesses and continue to stay in business.
- To add simplicity to your life. Giving a credit-card number over the telephone to book travel tickets, buy things by mail, or have flowers sent to someone special a thousand miles away sure beats driving to the bank to withdraw cash or waiting for checks to clear!

The key ingredient of the American financial system and others, as well, is *credit* that allows payments to be made toward items over a period of time that are not affordable in the present at their full cost. Through projected future income you are given the opportunity to use something in the present by agreeing to pay for the item plus interest over time.

Wisdom on Wealth

Credit is a valuable financial resource to draw from for everyone and frequently a major factor in the creation of dreams. Credit adds another dimension to the value of money, in a sense multiplying its value

Without the extension of credit to governments, businesses, and individuals, our economy as we know it would not exist. For those of us who use credit responsibly, it is very convenient and advantageous. For those of us who don't, it can spell disaster. Most people, if they were unable to pay for their home over many years in the form of a mortgage, would not be homeowners. How many of us can write checks for $100,000 or more? The answer is obvious. Many of us can't even buy cars with cash.

As of January, 1996, according to the Federal Reserve, the total consumer debt was $988 billion and no doubt will top a trillion by 1997. The average American's outstanding credit-card balance stands at $1,750 as mentioned in *Money* magazine in 1996, with household balances at nearly $4,000 according to Bankcard Holders of America. Just between Thanksgiving and Christmas of 1995, Americans charged up another $120 billion while 3.3 percent were overdue at least 30 days on their payments. Credit-card issuers are enjoying the ride, granting people ever higher limits while raking in the endless interest payments, further dividing people into two well-known categories: those who *pay interest* and those who *earn interest.*

For the majority of people, having credit is valuable; it will allow them to buy and use certain necessary items that are otherwise unaffordable. To demonstrate that you are worthy of having credit granted, you must be able to prove that you earn at least a certain level of income and savings, show documentation of paying bills on time, perhaps have responsibly had a checking account for a period of time, and have achieved a certain level of education.

It has been common practice for many years for credit-card issuers to approach only those young adults who are attending college. These issuing banks know that statistically the more education one has, the more income and, therefore, bill-paying capacity one will attain later on. Most people have a credit file established by credit bureaus that financial institutions both report information to and have access to, to determine your credit worthiness. If your credit file shows a history of paying a mortgage, bank loans, and credit cards on time, there is a higher chance that you can obtain more credit. But if it shows that you are having a hard time paying off such things in a timely manner or that you're actually neglecting to pay, then you most likely will be refused any further credit. Based on what you show on a credit application and what may already be available from credit bureaus, potential credit grantors will give you a risk-rating score, which tells them how to determine how much and what type of credit to give you.

Wisdom on Wealth

It is more to your advantage to have *no* credit than *bad* credit.

An unknown risk is less risky to a lender than a known high risk. Think about this. Would you be more likely to lend a friend money who had a reputation for not paying money back without a reasonable excuse or be more trusting of a friend whom you never had lent money to?

OBTAINING CARDS

Most credit-card interest rates are high—charging 14 percent to 21 percent as an annual percentage rate or APR. I consider the interest rate of little significance, for with the plan I'm sharing here, you will rarely let payments run late enough to pay any interest charges. However, you may as well receive a rate lower than that of another card that offers the same services.

To establish a credit history you can apply for a gasoline or department store card that is easier to qualify for than bank cards are. Once you use credit cards, a credit report starts forming in your name. One way to obtain a bank card such as VISA or MasterCard whether you have no credit or bad credit is to apply for a *secured card*. A secured card is backed by cash you place in an account with the bank who issues you the card. Typically, the potential cardholder deposits a modest sum of

$250 to $1,000—an amount equal to the credit line. The application fees for these cards can run as high as $50, though some are free.

Normally, if you can establish financial responsibility by paying card bills on time—12 to 24 months for those with no credit and 18 to 36 months for people with bad credit—you can receive your security deposit back and finally have a regular unsecured card. Just be sure to ask the bank you are dealing with if the credit you are trying to build will be reported to credit agencies as "secured." If so, then going through all this effort may not be worthwhile, for a secured card may not be viewed favorably. Many banks report the use of a secured card just like an unsecured one. Should you be unable to pay your bills with a secured card, the issuing bank has access to your deposit to cover the charges. And more delays will be involved when applying for further credit.

By the way, not everyone qualifies for such a card. Those who still have lingering problems to settle with the Internal Revenue Service (IRS), have not paid their student loans on schedule or their child support, or those who have been convicted of credit or bankruptcy fraud may not have a chance. And stay away from credit "doctors" or credit "repair" places that do little more than blemish your credit even more by charging hefty fees.

MAXIMIZE YOUR CARD

You never have to get a credit card that charges interest on purchases from the day the purchase is made. Many offer a 25-day grace period that is interest-free and will send you the bill in plenty of time to pay it off before finance charges are incurred. Be careful to pay promptly for some can nick you with late fees of $10 to $30 if your payment arrives even a day late. Card issuers will float the purchase of a $25,000 new car for those with a high credit limit, but if the card users merely take out a cash advance of $100, finance charges begin immediately. Tangible items are viewed very differently than cash in the financial world. Cash is seen as a direct loan, so it will not be provided interest-free for any amount of time beyond 24 hours, under most circumstances. Also, for security purposes, an item purchased with credit is more easily traced than cash. Checks issued by credit-card banks are interpreted the same as a cash advance, with interest accumulating immediately. At times these checks are quite useful, for example when one needs to make a purchase from a merchant who does not accept credit cards but does take checks.

On regular purchases, once you know the billing cycle of your card company, you can plan your credit-card spending accordingly. For example, let's assume that your credit-card issuer sends out its bills on the 15th of each month and gives you until the 10th of the next month to pay, interest-free. If you purchase a $2,500 computer system on the 15th of July, this amount will not appear on your bill until the August 15th billing and will not be charged any interest until September 10th. Therefore, you will own the computer system for free for seven to eight weeks, continuing to receive interest on your $2,500 during that time or giving you time to stash away more paychecks to ease the burden of paying. Planning to make purchases this way is perfectly legal.

Wisdom on Wealth

As long as you are not paying finance charges, delay paying *all* bills as long as possible, whether they are from credit-card companies, taxing authorities, or utilities. Let interest accrue in *your* name for as much time as you can before you part with your money.

The exceptions to these words of wisdom may be when your checking account pays no interest or when bonuses are given for advance payment.

TROUBLE WITH CARDS

Trouble with credit cards begins when those who use them start paying interest charges, in addition to the cost of the item being purchased. At the exorbitant interest rates that credit-card issuers charge (around 14 percent to 21 percent), this adds up *very fast*. When the bill comes, you have the option to pay off the balance in full, part of it, or the minimum due. It seems amazing that a bill for well over $1,000 can arrive with a minimum due of only 20-some dollars, but this arrangement is very similar to a home mortgage, in which primarily interest is paid up front. It is a fact that some cards require as little as 2 percent of the balance to be paid monthly! If all you paid was the minimum due each month, you would take years and years to pay for the item being charged and far more than double its original price. It is through this process that credit-card banks make a fortune, even though they absorb substantial losses because of fraud and support costly telephone help centers and billing operations. Many people are virtually being "eaten alive" by interest charges.

The way people bring themselves into more serious trouble is to pay low amounts due on such bills and continue charging. That way, your debt now compounds in more than one manner. Carried even further, if the minimums due become too difficult to pay on time, card banks threaten to cancel your card and your credit rating drops, of course making it harder to obtain more credit. However, you are still responsible for the bill and the card issuer may try to tack on collection fees as well. In the worst case, when it becomes clear to all parties involved that you will not be able to make payment, you may have to declare bankruptcy to be relieved of having to pay certain debts. Circumstances do occasionally arise because of a catastrophe or other situation that makes some bills unaffordable, regardless of how responsible one is. So bankruptcy does have its time and place, but should only be a last resort. Unfortunately, according to the Federal Reserve, more than one million bankruptcies were filed in the United States in 1996, the most ever in a year.

BANKRUPTCY—THE LAST RESORT

First of all, before filing for bankruptcy, make every attempt to work out arrangements *directly* with creditors. And put a stop to any harassment by debt collectors. You don't owe a collector *anything*, nor is there any legal requirement to deal with collectors. Should they bother you more than a few times, you can write a "cease-and-desist letter" to them that is considered a legal document and change your telephone number. By all means, never tell collectors you can pay if you can't and never tell them you can't if you can. Consumers are protected somewhat by the Fair Debt Collection Practices Act of 1977.

Times do arise when people are unable to compromise with creditors. When you have done all you can do in good faith to work out payment arrangements or have a debt discharged, your final resort is to file papers in bankruptcy court. In many circumstances you can fill out most of the papers yourself rather than creating more debt by hiring an attorney, though an initial consultation with a lawyer could be of value. Have your finances arranged *in advance* in such ways that creditors can't cause total devastation to your net worth. Promptly closing, transferring, or rearranging your finances far beyond the norm to hide your assets can be construed as fraud by a judge in a court of law and possibly lead to criminal prosecution.

Another legal procedure that can be implemented to force the payment of debts is the garnishment of your wages. Under some conditions you may be required to have your employer withhold a portion of each paycheck, normally not more than 25 percent, to pay off an obligation over time. You have the right to protest garnishment to have it reduced or eliminated. Another method some creditors can use to guarantee themselves some return is to place liens on your property, which when sold, entitles them to their portion.

CREDIT CARD EXTRAS? JUST SAY NO TO MOST

What people need is a card that is accepted in as many different locations as possible, has the standard grace period of at least 25 days without interest charges, provides revolving credit, permits partial payments to be made when necessary, has no annual fee, and perhaps carries some worthwhile perks. These perks may be rental-car collision insurance, rebates on purchases, and airline miles. I have a friend who saved more than $2,500 on the cost of a family trip from Texas to Canada through charging *everything* she would ordinarily buy.

Many banks offer "premium" or "prestige" cards under such names as "gold" or "platinum," with added extras such as extended warranties on purchases, legal advice, and medical assistance worldwide. My research clearly indicates that such perks are little more than inducements to consumers and hardly worthwhile when reality hits. I challenge you to find a good, English-speaking attorney in Madagascar when you are mistakenly thrown in jail, who honors your credit card as familiar card commercials have advertised. You are likely to have a similar experience with a doctor as well. As for extended warranties, by the time you narrow down all the exceptions to what is covered, pay to ship an item across the country so it can be verified as defective, and wait weeks and weeks, what's it all worth? It wasn't long ago that some major card banks were televising commercials that featured computers falling down stairways, dogs chomping on VCR wires, and thugs loading their van with cameras and TVs, with coverage up to $50,000. This protection has recently been reduced virtually to nothing. And these major card banks won't pay unless such occurrences are not already covered by homeowner's or renter's insurance, or by the one causing the loss, if clearly negligent. Even if these extras *were* as good as claimed by the card issuers, the typical person will not make use of them often enough to justify their higher annual fees. Remember that whether your card is gold, platinum, candy-cane striped, has your photograph on it (a good security idea), or the Mona Lisa's smile gazing back at you, its usefulness may be the same.

Also, watch out for credit-card literature in your mailbox that claims some outrageously low interest rate—as low as 5.9 percent—with no annual fee. The very low interest rate is normally a "teaser rate" to entice your business, which may last six months before being raised well into the teens, like other cards. And note the small print regarding the annual fee that will probably say "for the first year" after mentioning that there is no fee. I really laughed when I received a card solicitation that said there would be no annual fee for either the first year or the second year if I should enter the second year with a balance of at least $1,500. Of course, the interest on $1,500 will rapidly exceed most annual fees. Another amusing situation that parallels this example arose when a credit-card bank offered me a Christmas gift of not having to pay even the minimum payment for a month. The bank would have received the gift of more interest had I played that game.

Another clever credit-card incentive to keep you spending is the "pay-you-back" feature. It is very hard to significantly benefit from this concept because to be credited a significant sum, you must charge up such high amounts that you will be unable to pay off the balance in full within the first billing period. Interest charges on this fee more than offset the "pay-you-back" feature.

One amusing enticement a bank tried during 1995 was to offer potential customers full payback of all interest accrued on their cards *if* customers use the card for *20 years*. The bank lured 700,000 new customers with this offer!

Wisdom on Wealth

The bottom line remains: Avoid creating unnecessary debt and be among those who *earn interest instead of pay it*. Saving and investing all those interest charges over a 20-year period will put you ahead, with the right investment.

NEVER PAY FEES

Some credit cards have no annual fee but, instead, have a monthly fee billed each time the card user makes a purchase. Some have late payment fees or, worse yet, early pay-off penalties. Others have even more incentives to keep you charging away, such as lotteries, percentage donations to the Olympics or a charity, and discounted tickets to amusement centers such as Sea World, etc. Having a 1 in 1,855,968 chance to win $100,000, donating a couple of dollars to charity, or saving $10 on tickets is not worth *any* annual fee! Fees do add up. Over a 20-year period, at $25 annually, you will have parted with $500 that, when the opportunity, value or cost of that sum is taken into account, could easily be triple this amount. Another tactic to keep you paying high fees is to boost your sense of financial power by giving you a higher and higher line of credit. Once people are provided with $5,000 to $10,000 or more in credit, they tend to feel it is worth paying the $25 to $50 and up in annual fees, because many other card-issuing banks will treat them as total strangers with a very low credit limit. Incidentally, a number of card issuers charge fees of $10 to $50 for exceeding your limit, so do keep an eye on your purchases within a billing cycle.

Many card issuers try to entice cardholders into their shopper/buyer clubs, claiming that they offer better prices on lots of merchandise from TVs to cars. As an incentive to join, cheap merchandise such as calculators, pocket radios, or travel clocks frequently are given away. I have compared prices. They are not competitive and when one takes into account the membership fee of about $50 a year for most of them, forget it! Also, joining such clubs creates more temptation to spend, which, of course, is exactly what card issuers want. Get your free gadget and get out.

OTHER THINGS TO CONSIDER

Keep in mind that if your card is jointly held and doesn't waive the balance in case of death, the card-issuing bank has a right to come after the joint partner on the card, even if that other person never used the card. Unless the balance on a card in an individual's name was left very high (more than a few thousand dollars) and/or your easily accessed assets can have liens placed on them, card issuers normally will absorb the loss. So should you max out your credit line when the doctor says you only have six months to live? No. In addition to obviously being unethical, you might get charged with fraud, and issuers may be able to attach life-insurance proceeds and even some of your beneficiary's assets, if it can be shown that the beneficiary gained from this maneuver. Also, if significant collateral items are involved such as cars and furniture, issuers can repossess them.

Wisdom on Wealth

Keep in mind that if your card is jointly held and doesn't waive the balance in case of death, the card-issuing bank has a right to come after the joint partner on the card, even if that other person never used the card.

Another loss to the consumer is credit-card security protection at an additional $15 to $40 a year. Instead, protect yourself by doing the following:

- Limit the number of cards you carry.
- Keep personal identification numbers (PINs) imbedded in your nerve cells.
- Leave toll-free numbers to card companies written down in your car glove compartment and at home, so they can be contacted immediately to stop fraudulent use of your cards.
- Be smart about when and where you go while carrying credit cards.

These rules apply to other items in your wallet or handbag, and checkbook, too. Don't be a victim!

CARD PROBLEMS? YOU HAVE RIGHTS

Several types of errors can appear on credit-card bills for a variety of reasons. Usually, errors take the form of bills for items or services that you never purchased. When this happens you are under no obligation to pay. The opposite can also occur. I have an acquaintance who never received a MasterCard bill for a $450 camera purchased years ago. Clearly the camera store would have contacted him had they not been able to receive credit for the purchase, so a processing error occurred somewhere. One fact is certain and that is that someone—company or many individuals combined—bought that camera.

These are normally clerical mistakes made at the bank-card process-ing center. It was amusing to hear the caller on Talknet's Bruce Will-iams radio talk show a while back who claimed to have received a credit-card bill for $4,800 worth of purchases made in Paris when this person had hardly ever left the state of Ohio—let alone gone abroad! Cards are lost, stolen, and expired while unauthorized signatures, illegible transactions, and duplicate charge slips are processed. I have only been falsely billed on a credit card once in the 20 years I have had one, so I generally believe that such errors are rare. However, you should always carefully check bills when they come and know what to do if there is a problem.

Should you be billed for purchases you are sure you never made, receive defective merchandise, or very inferior service somewhere, you have legal rights to fight back. The Truth and Lending and Fair Credit Billing Acts protect the consumer and even permit charge-backs to the credit-card issuers and merchants. You must notify the card-issuing bank of any problems within 60 days of receiving bills of this type and the issuer must respond within 30 days with a resolution. A clear copy of the bill in question should be enclosed with a cover letter describing precisely what the error(s) are and should be sent by certified mail. Within a week you should follow up by telephone. Most card issuers solve these problems promptly. If disputed charges are for a substantial sum of money, merchants in question have to verify that they have no record of a transaction in your name. In a worst-case scenario in which high-level fraud is involved, things can get quite rough for a period of time. Normally, the worst thing that can happen to the consumer is a liability of $50 for all unauthorized charges and often even this is waived if the cardholder has a clean record with such matters.

Should you have the slightest hunch that a purchase you expect to make may be problematic and involve a refund, credit, or repairs, then making the purchase with a credit card is a wise move. There is no "Fair Cash Act" to protect you if you pay in cash or by check. In other words, shopping with a credit card offers the consumer more negotiat-ing power if problems arise. Some banks have been known to take cus-tomer charge-backs for up to six years after a purchase was made, though I believe such actions are very rare. I can just imagine the look on a merchant's face when a customer returns a VCR that looks like it has had masking tape instead of videotape run through its heads!

For further security protection, "smart cards" have been developed that have built-in chips, permitting merchants to instantly know stacks of information about the consumer—maybe more than many wish to have revealed. Considering that some chips now have the capacity to hold as much information as a 250-page book, I doubt that people want every cashier in the mall knowing their life stories.

CREDIT CARDS ARE CONVENIENT

As long as carrying a credit card does not tempt you to spend any more money than you would without the card, then you most certainly are an ideal candidate for a card. Credit cards are particularly convenient for traveling because you can pay for all of your purchases with one check, after arriving home. And hopefully you had paid vacation time that leaves you with another paycheck when you get back. I recommend leaving close to half or more of what you estimate your charges will be in the bank before you go, so that when the bill arrives it will be less of a burden to pay. Vacation or not, using a credit card for routine expenses is fine if you prefer not to use cash or write checks for every little expense during the month. Cards also are useful for calling in orders for far-away businesses you deal with to expedite service. You only need one or two cards, *ever*. With VISA and Master Card being the most widely accepted, find one of the two with the best deals and apply. Even for those who have serious reservations about credit and prefer to pay for everything by check, debit card, or in cash, it is still advisable to get a card and build up a couple of thousand dollars of credit in case of an emergency. For example, if you should suddenly have a family emergency and need $900 for plane tickets, and you don't have this extra amount in your bank account, you are stuck on the ground. Liquidating long-term investments or retirement funds for this purpose is not wise. At least if you have a credit card, you can pay for the tickets over a couple of months, if necessary. Also, using a credit card builds a credit report, which can help in future credit needs such as purchasing a home or anything else you wish to finance.

Many personal finance guides suggest having "three to six months' salary packed away" immediately accessible at a local bank. However, by establishing several thousands of dollars of credit on a credit card or two, you can use this source of instant money to pay for some unexpected bills. Credit is preferable than leaving a substantial sum in a bank account receiving less than 4 percent interest. True emergencies are rare and I believe rare enough to "take the risk" of not leaving much extra in the bank. Money should always be working for you, at least as hard as you work to get it. So choosing to leave thousands of dollars in a low-interest savings or checking account for the long-term is simply not using good judgment. In all likelihood, you probably have some level of insurance coverage for most major emergencies anyway. Of course, if the crisis is deep and lengthy, such as a layoff or disability, running up credit charges is not recommended, because paying them off may cause too much hardship. I hope at a time of such need you are not already in debt, may have a working spouse to help, can still find creative ways to earn money at least part-time, or discover that downsizing your lifestyle really isn't so bad after all.

14 SIMPLE RULES TO LIVE BY

1. Never apply for a card with an annual fee unless benefits such as air miles save you more than the combined cost of the fee over several years.
2. Be certain that your credit card always provides a 25-day grace period without late fee charges, other than interest.
3. Get cards with lower-than-average interest rates that stay that way.
4. Obtain cards that permit revolving credit, not ones that must be paid in full every month or debit cards.
5. Avoid cards that use previous balance calculation methods. The fine print with your card literature will tell you.
6. Don't apply for cards with added cash-advance and prepayment penalties.
7. Only get cards with extra features if they are truly free.
8. Get a card with worldwide acceptance.
9. Don't bother with shopper/buyer club memberships.
10. Be crime conscious and don't pay for card-protection plans.
11. Know how to respond fast if your card(s) are stolen.
12. Know how to handle improper charges you never made.
13. Realize what benefits and perks your card offers.
14. Use cards for convenience and emergencies when appropriate.

CREDIT REPORTS AND CREDIT BUREAUS

No matter where you are in your life, periodically obtaining a copy of your credit report is an essential aspect of sound financial management. You want to be sure there are no errors on your report or that someone is not making fraudulent use of your credit. Credit bureaus—three primary ones in the United States—are in the business of maintaining credit histories on millions of Americans. These agencies store credit information that is reported by subscribing credit grantors and collected from some public records. Credit grantors use credit reports when making credit-granting decisions. So having credit-reporting agencies saves grantors the time of finding the information themselves.

Wisdom on Wealth

No matter where you are in your life, periodically obtaining a copy of your credit report is an essential aspect of sound financial management.

A credit report simply contains information about loans, charge accounts, bankruptcies, tax liens, and judgments. The report does not contain personal information about your lifestyle, medical history, criminal history, personal assets, or net worth, race, religion, or income. Credit bureaus by law must be able to inform you about what business has made an inquiry into your credit record, if you request this information. The Fair Credit Reporting Act even permits employers to access your credit record. Some now use this option for it has been determined that financial responsibility often goes along with being responsible in other areas as well. Keep in mind that it is the law that negative information must be removed from your credit file within seven years, except for bankruptcies, which are kept for ten years.

ERRORS

Up to 30 percent of credit reports contain some level of error. Most tend to be minor with some in your favor and others not. Should you wish to dispute an item or two on your credit report, you may contact the credit bureau of choice, identify the problem, and provide a clear explanation and sometimes documentation as well. The credit bureau then will contact the grantor in question. This investigation can take up to two months. If the bureau is unable to resolve your dispute, you have the right to file your own explanation again. Send it via certified mail. Some errors are as minor as the misspelling of your name. The worst show balances due on bills that are not yours, bills you already paid off ages ago, or, worse yet, a bankruptcy you never filed for.

One of the more common problems is discovering that a grantor of a generous sum never reported it. In this case you can contact the grantor directly and request that your good credit be filed with the credit bureaus. And then contact all three credit bureaus to verify that they have placed this new record on your report.

It is simple to receive an updated copy of your credit report. All you do is call TRW at 800-682-7654, Transunion at 800-851-2674, or Equifax at 800-685-1111. They will request your proper name, all addresses of where you have lived the past five years, your Social Security number, date of birth, spouse's first name if married, copy of your current driver's license, and a recent utility bill or mortgage statement to verify your current address. At the time of this writing, Transunion and Equifax charge a nominal fee for a report.

IS YOUR CREDIT TOO GOOD?

Your credit can never really be *too* good. The only disadvantage of very good credit, which can be rectified, is having to deal with the constant flow of solicitation for more credit. Are you tired of receiving pre-approved credit-card applications in the mail? Had I wanted to, I could now have several hundred thousand dollars of credit if I applied and was accepted for all those cards and loans over the past few years. A 17-year-old high school student managed to obtain $300,000 of credit from responding to all the mailings he could get! A financial planner in California collects cards. He was featured in *Kiplinger's Personal Finance* magazine a few years ago and, by now, may have topped a million dollars in credit. Fortunately, the two people cited here simply created credit fortunes for curiosity's sake. I don't believe it is so easy to accomplish such feats now. Should you wish to stem the flow of credit solicitation, there is hope and it worked for me. You can write to Mail Preference Service, TRW Target Marketing Services Division, 910 North International Parkway, Suite 919, Richardson, TX 75081. In addition, you may order "Stop Junk Mail Forever" for only $2 from Good Advice Press, P.O. Box 78, Elizaville, NY 12523 and write to the Direct Marketing Association, PO Box 9008, Farmingdale, NY 11735. TRW's service will notify Equifax and Transunion. State that you want your name and address removed from mailing lists that are compiled for marketing purposes and supply your Social Security number. Junk mail wastes your precious time and energy, uses extra paper resources, and is a drag on the Postal Service.

A couple of agencies are very helpful in finding the best deal and in answering credit-card questions. These are the Bankcard Holders of America in Salem, Virginia at 800-553-8025, and for secured cards, Card Trak at 800-874-8999.

BORROWING AND LENDING

The whole concept of loaning money is based on *trust*. I avoid borrowing from or lending to anyone except those closest to me whom I can definitely trust Money lent but not trusted may as well be considered a gift.

Wisdom on Wealth

The whole concept of loaning money is based on *trust*.

When it comes to borrowing from an institution for a mortgage, car, home improvement, or education, it pays well to shop around. Getting to know your banker can help, but you still will have to qualify by having steady employment, a good credit history, or enough collateral in case you default on the loan. Collateral can be in the form of cash or the item being purchased with the loan such as a new car or home. A bank's decision to grant a loan will be based on the loan's intended purpose by the borrower. Financial institutions must be able to clearly define risk parameters before granting loans.

Robert Frost once said, "A bank is a place where they lend you an umbrella while the sun shines and ask for it back again when it rains." There is some truth in this, but in general our system of credit has created more opportunity and wealth for more people than any other in history.

Interest rates vary considerably, depending on what you intend to use loans for. Recently, my credit union was offering loans to take a vacation at 13.9 percent, but if I wanted to finance a new car I could have received a 6.5 percent loan. However, if the car I had wanted was used and more than five years old, I would have had to pay 12 percent.

Worse yet, one of the requirements of financing a car is to have *full insurance coverage* on the vehicle, a costly expense that might not be necessary if you paid in cash and could determine the extent of your coverage. To purchase the computer I am using to type this book I faced the options of borrowing from the bank at 12 percent, paying it off at 11.5 percent on the same bank's credit card, or following up on a teaser rate offer received by mail for only 5.9 percent. Unfortunately, those least able to pay and probably only able to buy a used car must pay higher rates and full insurance coverage because they are labeled a higher credit risk.

Often the greater the amount loaned, the lower the interest rate that can be offered. Usually, the actual dollar amount of profit from the loan is still high enough to satisfy the lender. Exceptions exist, however, including "jumbo mortgage loans," those more than $200,000 in which extra fees and/or higher interest rates are applied for no good reason other than profits.

For more versatility, consider borrowing on your home equity (not legal in Texas because of the homestead exemption law), the interest on which, as of 1996, is tax deductible. Another option, which is the least recommended, is to take out a loan against your employer 401(k), 403(b), or profit-sharing plan. In this case you are borrowing against yourself. Except for *home* loans that can be stretched out for 30 years, retirement plan loans must be paid back within five years or else you face a significant tax penalty. The reason I don't think highly of these loans is that people cut heavily into their future savings by losing years of tax-deferred compounding, adding up to big bucks by retirement age.

Cash value life insurance policies are another source to borrow from. You are permitted to borrow up to 95 percent of accumulated cash savings in such policies, with the clear understanding that whatever outstanding balance you owe is subtracted from the death benefit of the policy. If you are borrowing from a life insurance policy, have your agent supply written information on how future accumulations in the policy will be affected. You also may take out a margin loan against stocks and bonds you have through a brokerage firm such as Merrill Lynch or Charles Schwab, and use the money for anything you want. Keep in mind, however, that if the stock market crashes, you may be asked to post more securities or cash as collateral to support the loan.

Using Other People's Money (OPM) is what millions of people regularly engage in to buy homes or cars, take vacations, start businesses, and for a host of other financial needs. Without credit, the lives of hundreds of millions of people would virtually come to a standstill. You should not be afraid to borrow when it clearly will affordably be to your advantage to have a more prosperous life in the present than would otherwise take many years to pay for in cash. However, as you age it is best to place yourself in a more and more secure position by reducing outstanding debt and ultimately eliminating it. Hopefully, by then, you will be among those who *earn* interest, instead of incur it.

The bottom line is clear. Wise use of credit and banking can save you money and greatly add to the quality of your life. Just avoiding most bank service charges and credit-card fees and interest payments is a savings of several hundred dollars a year for a typical account holder, *thousands* of dollars over many years with an investment potential of thousands more. But the real benefit of credit is its ability to expand not only the quality of your life but increase your prosperity as well. By borrowing money to start a business you may be the next Sam Walton or Bill Gates. Yes, it can be worth spending money to borrow money to receive far more money back.

Wisdom on Wealth

Wise use of credit and banking can save you money and greatly add to the quality of your life.

CHAPTER 6

Saving a Fortune in Rent or Mortgage Payments

Rent or mortgage payments, in all likelihood, make up the most costly part of your budget. Generally, people are willing to pay a lot to have a secure, comfortable space that is theirs to sleep in, decorate as they wish, and spend time engaging in whatever activity they want. To many, their housing is an extension of who they are. Through years of dealing with housing costs under a variety of conditions, I discovered numerous alternative strategies that have saved my household a fortune. Here are just a few.

SAVING WITH RENTING STRATEGIES

Before renting any property it is essential to set a realistic upper limit of what you will spend on housing each month. This self-imposed limit will permit you to save extra cash. When considering ways to limit your renting costs, ask yourself these basic questions:

- If the rent includes utilities, how much assumed utility usage is added into the rent and might it be cheaper to directly control my utility spending?
- Will an apartment suffice for now instead of a house?
- Can I tolerate having a roommate or two for the time being?

- Am I temporarily able to deal with living in a less-than-ideal neighborhood?
- Can I live in a smaller-than-average place?
- Will my rental manager let me sign a longer-term lease to lock out any rent increases, stopping inflation dead for this period?

If renting, perhaps you can pay off part or all of your rent by working part-time in the rental office or performing some maintenance work. Many years ago we house-sat for an entire summer in beautiful Washington, D.C., while the owners were in Europe, saving ourselves money on housing costs. Some college students have saved many thousands of dollars in rent assisting an elderly or handicapped home-owner, baby-sitting, housekeeping, cooking, caring for pets, helping a child with homework, painting, landscaping, or helping with a family business. Sometimes rent will be lowered if you find someone to rent a vacant space for your landlord or improve the property. Just $150 a month off your rent for six hours of work per week is $5.77 per hour, $1,800 extra per year, or $9,000 in five years, which, if well invested, could increase your wealth by $15,000. Some deals of this type are subject to income taxes by the IRS as "bartering transactions," though rarely are such relatively small amounts reported or pursued by the IRS. Certain domestic positions can be real career opportunities. We once were offered a position that included a salary of $38,000 a year, spacious private housing, free utilities and food, a free car and gas, paid vacations, and insurance to assist in the caretaking of a large estate. Many of the "work-off-your-rent" strategies can be found advertised in newspapers, especially in college towns.

RENTING VERSUS BUYING

Chances are that if you are just entering the work force, you do not have down payment money to buy a home yet, but at some point, you will likely face the question of whether to keep renting or to own. The following may help you to decide:

- Do you want to own property to live in or as an investment?
- How long do you plan to live in the area? If less than a year or two, you may want to consider continuing to rent despite the feeling that it's "money out the window" every month. The costs associated with buying and home improvements are extensive and only financially justifiable if you're willing to do what it takes to

sell at a good profit. Also, because of how mortgages are amortized, during the first few years homeowners lose money in interest payments.

- Are housing costs level, rapidly rising, or on their way down in your area? If costs are skyrocketing, buy as soon as you reasonably can, though don't expect much appreciation on the house after your purchase if the market has been high for a while. If prices are stable, buy when you are very comfortably able to do so. If prices are going down, delay your purchase and investigate why this is occurring. If you are satisfied the reasons are legitimate, try to get the best deal you can find. Watch out, however, if you sense that it is because of a rapidly declining job market.

Buying a home is the most expensive purchase you ever will make as a consumer. Consider the money, time, and energy you need to maintain a property, keep up repairs, and yard work, plus all the initial purchase costs versus the convenience of renting, where you can simply pick up the telephone when the toilet floods. That's why most experts recommend that you accumulate a lump savings equivalent to at least three to six months of your take-home salary, in addition to the cost of the down payment and other initial home-buying expenses. Even if you have the money you need to buy a new home, you will want additional cash to decorate, landscape the garden, and perhaps purchase additional furniture.

Wisdom on Wealth

Buying a home is the most expensive purchase you ever will make as a consumer.

Common sense might convince you that renting is cheaper than owning, so is buying a house really worthwhile? When one is ready for the commitment and responsibility of ownership, owning a house is to your advantage. Here's why:

1. First, you have the benefits of leverage. For example, you may have put down only $10,000 on a $100,000 house, but the appreciation you will get over time is on the full $100,000. In other words, if you get only a 3 percent gain in a year on the value of your home, you're actually receiving a 30 percent gain on the

$10,000, an excellent annual rate of return and precisely how a number of real estate investors have become wealthy.

2. Inflation can work *for* you instead of *against* you. This is because your mortgage payment is locked in for the term of the mortgage. As inflation rises along with your income, your mortgage becomes an increasingly smaller percentage of your cost of living.

3. The opportunity value of money is tremendous. For example, $25,000 used as a down payment and closing costs for a $110,000 house has the potential to grow to $50,000 in just over seven years, if you receive an average annual return of 10 percent. With certain very aggressive growth stocks, you could do far better or far worse as you run up against the law of risk and reward explained further in Chapter 11. Doing some basic calculations to fit your own circumstances is essential while understanding that the relative value of a dollar projected into the future cannot be guaranteed. Several software programs are available, including some excellent ones from Dearborn Financial Publishing, Inc., in Chicago, the publisher of this book.

INTEREST IS EXPENSIVE

Because of how interest is calculated, a $100,000 home could cost more than $275,000 over the life of a 30-year mortgage. If you buy a house with cash, you would have no mortgage payments and a wonderful feeling of financial empowerment, but this is only a wise choice if you are wealthy enough to comfortably enjoy this luxury. Because most of us cannot afford to buy homes with cash, lenders have created a system in which monthly payments with interest charges permit millions of people to afford houses, and millions of lenders to reap the rewards with a high profit for themselves.

Your mortgage loan contract should provide the option to pay off the mortgage early, without penalties, and there are conditions in which doing so is to your advantage. Because of the way financial institutions design mortgage loans, buyers pay far more in interest than principal (the actual purchase price of the house) over the life of the loan. If you pay even a small additional amount each month, besides your regular payment toward the principal, you can save many thousands of dollars in interest costs, as well as reduce the time it takes to pay off the mortgage. If you're going to make extra principal payments, by far the most lucrative time is during the first five years, when more than 90 percent of your required payment merely goes to interest. Recently, a number of banks have become involved in offering to help homeowners pay their mortgage off early by acting as a third-party payer. They charge an initial fee of $300 to $400 plus monthly service charges to make your payments twice a month, or whatever other arrangement may suit the homeowner. Why pay for this service when your own mortgage company probably will accept extra payments from you anytime? Another reason to pay off a mortgage early, at least in the state of Texas where there is a 100 percent (set at less in other states) homestead exemption, is to protect assets from various types of creditors. Paying off your mortgage initially sounds great but is not always the best decision if you look at it closely. Perhaps the extra cash you apply to unrequired principal payments will earn you more money invested elsewhere, at a higher rate of return than most mortgage rates. If you can average a 12 percent return annually on your savings, then paying off an 8 percent mortgage early is not necessarily the wisest choice. Though being mortgage-free may be a great relief, if you can profit more by investing your money elsewhere, don't pay it off.

Just $50 a month added to a $600 monthly payment could chop close to ten years off a 30-year mortgage and save a bundle in interest.

Unfortunately, while your maximum benefit is during those first critical years, adding payments may be more difficult when new house expenses are typically higher initially, and you probably aren't at your peak earning potential. Later, by the time you have moved up in earnings, bought all your furniture, and replaced the roof and air-conditioning system with enough disposable income to increase your mortgage payments, adding to payments on the principal will not reap you anywhere near the benefits. In fact, if the first five years (which is your window of opportunity) have passed, you are nearly certain to receive far higher gains by investing your extra money elsewhere.

Of course, most mortgage companies will offer other options than the standard 30-year loan. If you can swing the higher payments, you can negotiate a shorter-term mortgage. Adjustable rate mortgages (ARMs) fluctuate with interest rates with a ceiling that can get quite painful if rates go up significantly. I usually don't recommend them for they add a risk component to your financial plan. Keep in mind, however, that ARM loans can be negotiated as convertible to a fixed rate for a fee. More rarely, there are balloon mortgages in which years pass with small, affordable payments, culminating in several-thousand-dollar payments later on. This type of mortgage could work for someone who is sure to get a windfall and/or move up the career ladder down the road.

With major changes in interest rates, homeowners can also refinance their mortgages to benefit from lower rates. Generally, financial planners recommend not refinancing a mortgage unless you can obtain a rate at least 2 percent less than your existing loan, because of the closing charges on the new loan.

As an incentive to keep the housing market alive and healthy, as well as to lighten the burden on homeowners, the IRS allows mortgage interest to be deducted on Schedule A. With lower interest rates in recent times and the rise in the standard deduction, however, the mortgage deduction has lost its luster for many people. I benefited from mortgage deductibility for only the first couple of years of owning my home before the standard deduction exceeded all Schedule A deductions, though my deductions are rather modest.

SEVEN EASY WAYS TO SAVE ON YOUR MORTGAGE

1. When applying for your mortgage, you will be told by the lending institution what interest rate it is offering. This is when you need to negotiate for a lower rate. Call around to other companies to compare rates and other closing costs. Even getting the rate down just a quarter of a point can save a couple of thousand dollars over the life of the loan.
2. Put down a larger-than-required down payment.
3. Add extra principal payments regularly, especially during the first five years.
4. Buy only the square footage of housing and yard space you need, keeping in mind that smaller houses have smaller mortgages, cost less to maintain, cost less to insure, and have a lower tax burden.
5. Consider the costs of paying more points at closing for a lower interest rate.
6. Compare costs of payments on 30-year, 25-year, 20-year, 15-year, and 10-year mortgages.
7. Do not purchase mortgage insurance or mortgage life insurance. If mortgage insurance is required, get out of paying it or obtain a prorated refund as soon as possible.

HOMEBUYING NEGOTIATIONS

Looking for a house to buy can be an exhausting exercise. Finding your dream home with all those ideal characteristics may not be possible. Even after you've narrowed down your choices and selected the home you want, you'll still be forced to consider that you're going to want the lowest price you can get while the seller wants the highest price. Always offer a low bid to start, normally 5 percent to 10 percent less than the asking price. The seller will counter your offer and you will counter the seller's until compromise is reached on by both sides. Normally, real estate transactions are mediated by a REALTOR®, though owner financing can bypass the costly commission charged by REALTORS® (some REALTORS® will discount their commissions) and permit the buyer to get a better deal.

When buying a home, you have to consider various fees. Among them are the following:

- Application and origination fees for items such as credit checks can cost $50 or more (Can you call TRW and have your free copy sent directly to the lender?)
- A title search for $75 that, if it's worth your time, you can do in your county courthouse
- Tax transfer fees at another $100 to $200
- Septic tank and termite certification at about $100 or more
- A survey that may cost another couple of hundred dollars
- Attorney's fees that, for a basic contract, can be as low as $25
- A prorated portion of property taxes

You may be able to avoid most of these fees by negotiating directly with the seller, filling out your own blank real estate contract, and spending the basic consultation fee to have an attorney look it over.

REDUCING SOME COSTS

For those who wish to lower or eliminate their big rent or mortgage payments, here are some suggestions for alternative strategies:

- If you have the disposition to handle being a landlord, you may consider purchasing a multifamily dwelling. This way you can receive a substantial portion of your mortgage cost in rent minus taxes.

- You could rent out a room in your home to a responsible person.
- Turn your garage into an efficiency apartment complete with a small stove, refrigerator, and basic furnishings. This could provide economical living for anyone and might be ideally suited for an aging relative. Modifying and installing appropriate plumbing and electrical needs could be somewhat costly initially but collecting $200 to $400 a month in rent would quickly pay this off. After a year or so you will be able to use this rental income to supplement your income. Also, most of these permanent improvements to your home will translate into increased value and tax deductions when the home is sold.

The burden of housing payments can be reduced as low as you want, depending on what you can offer other than cash. The renting option can be a great way for college students, young people getting started financially, and some singles or couples who prefer this way of life. For those who are settled into dependable employment and expect to remain in the same area for at least a few years, owning your own home is a wise choice. However, I hope you now understand the exceptions to this rule. And that you realize that paying off your mortgage early can never hurt, but under some circumstances alternatives may increase your wealth even more.

Wisdom on Wealth

For those who are settled into dependable employment and expect to remain in the same area for at least a few years, owning your own home is a wise choice.

CHAPTER 7

Winning with Insurance Strategies

Insurance policies are nothing more than risk contracts, contracts for which you pay an insurance company in exchange for lowering the chance of financial hardship in your or someone else's life. The most popular forms of insurance include health, death, disability, automobile, homeowner's, accident, and liability. Normally, the greater the value of assets being insured and the higher the risk of loss, the more costly the insurance will be. That's common sense. The challenge is in estimating your risk under various circumstances and estimating when you need insurance, what type, and how much. It would help to have access to the tables insurance companies use for determining these costs. Unfortunately, insurance companies keep this information secret. Enough statistics are available, however, to come up with a number of firm assumptions, the first of which is that, with few exceptions, insurance companies are earning enormous profits. The question then is whether it's worthwhile to give your money to insurance companies that will only help them increase these profits, while decreasing yours.

We all live every moment with risk. Unexpected things happen. My computer could blow up in my face as I am writing this sentence or I could suddenly slump over my keyboard with a heart attack. But I know the likelihood of either of these occurrences is highly improbable. So how much are we willing to compensate for risk by purchasing insurance and what can we do, as individuals, to further decrease risk in our lives?

Wisdom on Wealth

Insurance policies are nothing more than risk contracts, contracts for which you pay an insurance company in exchange for lowering the chance of financial hardship in your or someone else's life.

LIFE OR DEATH INSURANCE?

Do you wish to insure your life prosperity and energy or protect yourself from the heavy financial burdens that occur when someone dies? Life insurance is based on the assumption that families have one primary wage earner, whose income, if lost, causes financial catastrophe to the security of the family. This assumption has been altered in the past few decades, for the majority of families now have more than one source of income. Even in two-income households, however, the family depends on both incomes to support its lifestyle. If either person should die, one income alone may not be enough to support the household.

If you are single with no dependents, you can breeze through this section, because you probably need no life insurance. But if you are married and/or have dependent children, and are considering whether you need to buy insurance, keep in mind that through economizing your household finances, your cost of living will decrease significantly while your capacity to save will increase. This is important because the less costly your lifestyle, the less likely the loss of a spouse can devastate your household financially. Before buying insurance you should also consider your various sources of income. You might start by figuring out how much money you are entitled to from the government should you or your spouse pass away. In the event of death, when children under the age of 16 are involved, Social Security will pay spousal benefits (the age limit is extended for disabled children). Children themselves are also entitled to receive additional benefits up to the age of 19 and two months if they are still in school, subject to the family's income level. I have calculated that if my spouse were to pass away, Social Security benefits alone would cover about two thirds of all expenses for me and my son.

Another income source to consider is your pension plan, which, assuming you are vested, pays a spousal death annuity. In addition, all other retirement funds, including IRAs, 401(k)s, and defined-contribution plans, become accessible to your spouse on your death. Perhaps you and your partner have investments that you can tap into? Insurance agents now recommend people buy more than ten times their annual income in death benefits. Frankly, this is absurd most of the time. In addition, when estimating, you should subtract the costs of living for the deceased and factor in the far lower tax burden you will have to pay, because of your decreased income.

When you take into account all of these situations, you may find you won't require nearly so much life insurance as you originally had thought or were told by a salesperson. The only people who need a lot of life insurance are those who don't have built-in savings, Social Security benefits, or other sources of income, as well as those who are wealthy and know how to manipulate insurance to their financial advantage. Generally, you need life insurance during the period in your life when your beneficiaries, normally your spouse and/or children, would suffer undue financial hardship without your income. In addition to replacing daily living costs, you may want to maintain a substantial policy or two in the household to cover future major expenses such as paying off your mortgage, college educations, and uninsured medical expenses, though hopefully you are already doing some planning to take care of these expenses.

For those earning very modest incomes, life insurance simply should not be a high priority. With limited funds available, consider a major medical policy before spending on life insurance. If you are young and healthy and can't afford to *pay yourself* money each month to build your savings and investments, then insurance can wait.

Now that I have started you thinking about whether or not you need life insurance, let's look at what type of insurance is the most cost-effective. There are two basic types of life insurance with numerous variations on these themes. One is called term insurance, which covers the insured for a specified time period, and the other is called permanent insurance or whole-life insurance, which one can retain until one's death. Whole-life and related insurance have savings plans built into the policy, while term insurance is strictly coverage.

WHOLE LIFE: THE EXPENSIVE OPTION

Generally, I do not recommend the purchase of whole life, also known as cash value insurance. These policies are far too costly with too large a portion of your premiums applied toward sales commissions and various service charges. And the savings portion of these policies have typically low interest rates comparable to other higher-returning secure investments, and usually will not break even with inflation.

A similar type of policy, universal life insurance, also is not a great option, other than the flexibility it affords you to vary your premium amount over time. Recently, policies have been designed with better investment options for cash savings, now called variable life insurance. While these policies are significant improvements, they still don't compare to strictly buying death coverage and investing on your own.

For example, a typical whole or variable policy with a death benefit of $100,000 costs nearly $1,100 a year in premiums for a 35-year-old, nonsmoking man, while the purchase of death-only coverage or term insurance can be as little as a third of this sum. For those who have been paying premiums on a whole-life policy for many years, it may not be worth canceling it. You may at least be able to switch the cash value portion into a more aggressive investment, turning the policy to variable. Whole-life policies normally come with the option to borrow against the cash value portion, also not a good deal, for you are borrowing your own money from overpriced premiums you paid. If anything is owed on the loan at the time of your death, this amount is subtracted from your total. Another option may be to transfer the cash value into a self-directed annuity that can provide regular cash payouts. Policies that permit these exchanges are called convertible policies.

NEED LIFE INSURANCE? BUY TERM

As mentioned previously, premiums for term insurance are far less expensive because you are purchasing only death protection. So if you are not already knee-deep in a cash policy, seek out term. Two types of term policies are available: renewable and nonrenewable. Renewable policies permit you to renew your coverage without a physical exam until the age of 70, while nonrenewable policies require a medical exam after a set period of time, usually ten years. If you pass the exam, the policy permits renewal at a preferred price.

You can buy term insurance as "annual renewable," which simply means that the premium you pay rises each year you age to compensate for your increased risk of death. Or you can buy "level term," which means that the premium cost remains the same for a set period of time, such as 5, 10, or 15 years, while the death benefit decreases. If the price increases in level-term policies because of regulatory changes, as expected, annual renewable may be the best deal. In addition, this policy is attractive because you can adjust your premium based on changes in need. So, renewing each year assures your beneficiary of receiving exactly the death benefit you choose.

"Hybrid" or "blended" policies also attempt to combine some of the benefits of both cash value and term, which I don't recommend, largely for the same reasons I have against purchasing cash value policies in the first place. Maximize your value through purchasing straight term insurance.

RIDERS

One technique I use to help save money on insurance is to avoid riders. Most riders are merely features that agents may talk you into tacking on to your policy. Often they are costly and unnecessary. Here are a few examples of the most common riders and their setbacks:

- *Waiver of premium* permits you to stop paying premiums while keeping your coverage in the event that you become disabled and can't work. But this rider normally does not apply unless you have been disabled for at least six months, severely reducing its usefulness.
- *Guaranteed insurability* gives policyholders the right to buy another policy or more coverage without showing evidence of good health. Many policies place limits on the time of this guarantee, however, frequently making it invalid around the age of 50, right when you might need it most. Remember, also, the need for life insurance tends to decrease as time passes.
- *Accidental death or "double-indemnity"* rider pays twice the death benefit if you die in an accident. If you want twice as much coverage, buy it to begin with.
- *Living needs benefit* allows you to access the death benefit before your death, when a doctor certifies that you are terminally ill and probably will die within a year. Normally, you buy life insurance

to provide for your beneficiaries. Because your hospital bills generally will be covered by your health insurance, the only reason why you might want access to this windfall is to finally achieve some lifelong dream, such as taking a tour around the world with your closest of friends or family, while you're still well enough to enjoy it. Also, remember that if you receive your death benefits before your death, they are considered taxable income.

RATES

After you have created a thorough list that determines exactly how much insurance you think you might need, here are some resources to call to compare rates:

1.   Quotesmith, 800-556-9393
2.   Best Quote, 800-896-8006
3.   Term Quote, 800-444-8376
4.   Select Quote, 800-343-1985
5.   USAA, 800-531-9093

These companies, among others, provide computerized lists of competitive rates for many of the top-rated term insurance companies for free. All you do is give them a few simple facts over the telephone and they will answer most questions very competently. Though they may follow up by mail, no salespeople will call. With information from each and using a calculator, you may consume some time but it's well worth it when you find a really great rate. Rates for exactly the same coverage can vary from company to company by as much as 30 percent. Also, note that in Florida and California, life insurance companies are permitted to refund up to 75 percent of sales commissions on policies. They require that buyers of policies be present at the time of purchase, even if the buyer is just traveling through. Though legal in these states, it's difficult to find life insurance companies there that will provide this money-saving strategy.

To ensure that your application for insurance won't be rejected, you can receive a copy of the standard report most companies use to evaluate your eligibility by contacting the Medical Information Bureau (MIB) at PO Box 105, Boston, MA 02112, 617-426-3660. These reports typically contain information about your character, reputation, personal characteristics, health, employment record, finances, driving record, use of drugs or alcohol, sports and hobby interests, marital status, and more as it relates to how risky you may be to insure. Of course, health insurance companies use this information as well.

SOME FINAL THINGS TO CONSIDER

Let's review now the factors you should assess when considering life insurance:

- First, estimate how your household budget would change after the death of an income earner.
- Next, determine how much of a shortfall your household income will suffer. That is the figure on which you base your life insurance needs, minus any government or employer-provided coverage.
- Then call several of those companies I list, find the best quote, and pick a term policy to suit your needs.
- And last but not least, keep in mind that through applying well-disciplined lifestyle and investment philosophies while you are young (generally still in your 20s), you can reduce or perhaps eliminate the need for life insurance during those prime years of greatest financial responsibility.

HEALTH INSURANCE: POTENTIALLY YOUR WORST FINANCIAL BURDEN

As we all know, the costs of medical care have become nothing other than absurd during the past 20 years. Two minutes with a doctor now costs what a lower-wage earner takes home in a full day's work. Add on a lab test or two and a drug prescription and you may have gone through more than a week's salary. Be hospitalized for a day and watch a whole month's hard work vanish. Have major surgery and perhaps never be able to pay for it. Just what is the $5- to $20-per-hour worker supposed to do to be rid of the fear of financial catastrophe from becoming ill or getting hurt? With the cost of health care in 1997 estimated to be about a trillion dollars a year in the United States, the crisis is far from over.

What can you do to dramatically reduce your risks of major illness and injury while saving a fortune and feeling great? First of all, the maintenance of optimum health is a lifestyle philosophy derived, in part, from habits you formed in childhood, feelings of high self-esteem, and a daily awareness of what parts of your mind and body need to be stimulated. Our brain tells us when something is not healthy, often by signaling thirst, fatigue, excess cold or heat, hunger, fears, frustration, pain, symptoms of illness, and many other feelings. Unfortunately, many of us take our health for granted with the passage of time and have not learned to key into these signals and respond to them on a timely basis. Nor do many of us keep up with the latest findings in basic medical science.

In addition, such unhealthy habits as smoking, which, according to the Centers for Disease Control, kills more people a year than the number of accidents, suicides, alcohol abuse, and addictive drugs combined, make it difficult to maintain our ideal state of health. Smokers pay far more for life and some types of health insurance, cost nonsmokers higher health insurance rates, and pollute the environment and the air. As for their budget, according to the Center for Corporate Health Promotion, smokers typically spend about $600 a year for this bodily toxin, plus more for their medical care.

Wisdom on Wealth

For most people, good health can become a way of life because with proper maintenance, the body is almost perfectly designed to remain in excellent health for more than seven decades.

Obesity is another prevalent health risk. Those who were born with the ability to burn off calories quickly have little to be concerned with. But many people must make a conscious effort to maintain their ideal weight. It has been shown that overweight people can reset their metabolic rate, the rate at which the body uses energy, by stepping up their exercise on an almost daily basis. Aside from helping you to look and feel better, getting into proper physical condition can save you countless sums of money in reduced medical needs. And avoiding and/or learning healthier methods of dealing with stress—anger toward others we depend on such as a supervisor or spouse being the worst—is another major preventive action to take. For now, reduce the stress on your pocketbook. And keep in mind that by making less money available to the health care system, you are doing your part to keep downward pressure on prices.

METHODS OF SAVING A FORTUNE
ON HEALTH CARE

For most people, good health can become a way of life because with proper maintenance, the body is almost perfectly designed to remain in excellent health for more than seven decades. Practicing healthy habits is not only important to your longevity, but to your wallet! Following are more than 60 tips that will help you cut costs and save money on health care.

1. Don't visit the doctor for illnesses that take care of themselves or that you can easily manage yourself, such as common colds and minor stomach upsets.
2. Don't spend the money for a physical exam every year unless you have a chronic medical problem. From ages 20 to 40 every five years is adequate, from ages 40 to 65 every two years, and after 65, go once a year.
3. Do not assume that you must have a specific type of testing because your doctor presented no alternatives, which may cost less. Ask.
4. Inquire about costs of treatment while consulting your doctor. If the doctor is not comfortable discussing finances, consider getting another doctor.
5. When a charge appears to be too high, attempt to negotiate. Often a bill will be reduced. If a medical establishment refuses to negotiate, you may want to play hardball and simply send it a check for less with a letter explaining why.
6. Become informed about what fees are reasonable by checking with your insurance company, calling your local medical board and hospital business offices.
7. Get any medical procedures or treatments performed *outside* the hospital, if possible. The same procedure can cost triple what it would cost in your doctor's office.
8. Establish a relationship with a doctor who, over the telephone, offers remedies for minor problems and occasionally is trusting enough to write prescriptions.

9. Obtain the free opinion of nurses at medical clinics by telephone or visit your local pharmacist who may know of an over-the-counter remedy.

10. Look for free tests, screenings, flu shots, and immunizations for children that are sponsored by area hospitals, major employers, or your state health department.

11. Are you near a medical or dental school? Some offer certain types of treatment and tests at much reduced rates.

12. Try to negotiate for a flat rate for several procedures to be performed at the same time.

13. Purchase a couple of self-care and preventive-care books that describe most common symptoms, how to treat them, and when intervention by a medical professional may be necessary.

14. Never use emergency rooms (ERs) except for real emergencies that are life-threatening such as heart attacks, major injury, shock reactions to allergens or toxins, or bleeding you can't control. Treatment in the ER is charged at an exorbitant rate over the doctor's office rate.

15. Use home test kits. They are available for pregnancy, ovulation, colorectal cancer, glaucoma, strep throat, and urinary-tract infections. A home AIDS test is around the corner.

16. Shop wisely for vitamin and mineral supplements. For example, one name brand of a 600-milligram daily dose of calcium to prevent osteoporosis can cost more than $700 a year while a generic equivalent can cost under $60, and calcium carbonate powder to sprinkle in your food costs about $20 a year.

17. Consider alternative medicine for some conditions such as herb treatment, homeopathy, acupuncture, and specific recommendations for exercising and dietary changes. Even minor changes in one's emotional/psychological well-being can reduce or eliminate major illnesses.

18. When you must be hospitalized, check out as soon as possible. Beat the checkout time the next morning if you must stay over or you may be billed hundreds of more dollars for another day.

19. Bring your own medications to the hospital to avoid the outrageous overcharges that can be more than 150 times your cost at your pharmacy.

20. When hospitalized, maintain a diary of all procedures, drugs taken, doctor visits, and the times of all these events. If you are too incapacitated, arrange for someone you trust to keep these

records. You will need these records to compare to the hospital bills.

21.   Scrutinize your hospital and doctor bills, even if insurance is covering them. According to an article in the April, 1996, issue of *Glamour* magazine, Charles Inlander, president of the People's Medical Society in Allentown, Pennsylvania (backed by a survey conducted by Congress's General Accounting Office), almost 90 percent of bills have errors, 80 percent of which are not in the patient's favor. If the bills become overwhelming and appear to be outrageous, consider using a service such as Med Review in Austin at 800-397-5359 to check them out.

22.   Keep in mind your right to informed consent, the right to understand and agree to various procedures.

23.   To avoid duplicate testing in the hospital, be sure your doctor has passed along any results of tests previous to hospitalization, as well as relevant records.

24.   Don't visit an ophthalmologist for vision problems when an optometrist can probably diagnose and treat the problem for up to 50 percent less.

25.   Obtain a copy of your eyeglass or contact-lens prescription and then shop around for an optician whom you can deal with directly, which can save around 30 percent.

26.   Order contact lenses by mail in bulk if you wear disposables. Try Lens Direct 800-772-5367 (also discounts on sunglasses) and Contact Lens Specialists 800-422-8489.

27.   Be alert when handling contact lenses. Don't buy contact-lens insurance.

28.   When a doctor recommends expensive medical treatment, get a second opinion.

29.   Ask your doctor about generic alternates for prescriptions that can cost half as much as brand names. This is often true of over-the-counter medications as well, which you can consult your pharmacist about.

30.   Compare the prices of buying prescription drugs by mail from such places as Medi-Mail 800-331-1458, Action Mail Order 800-452-1976, and AARP 202-434-7990 (members only).

31.   If you live near Mexico, go across the border with your prescription and save 50 percent to 80 percent. For example, a bottle of 90 ten-mg tablets of Valium that sells for $138 in the United States costs only $8.75 in Mexico, while 28 pills of

Prozac that retails in this country for $70 is priced at just $31.60 in Mexico. Save on dental treatments and eyeglasses as well.

32. Take medications you really need. Many doctors overprescribe. For example, you may be given a pain killer after minor surgery when aspirin may work fine.

33. Compare prices at your local stores of vitamin and mineral supplements with purchasing them by mail from Mail Away Vitamins, 800-645-2929.

34. Lost your job or relocating without insurance? The Consolidated Omnibus Budget Reconciliation Act (COBRA) is a federal law that permits you to extend employer coverage for up to 18 months (27 months if you are also eligible for Social Security disability), if you work for a company with at least 20 employees. However, you are required to pay the *entire* premium yourself. With typical group managed-care plans charging employers from around $200 a month for individual coverage per employee and up to $800 for family coverage, more than half of which the employer usually pays, COBRA can be prohibitively expensive to many, especially those who have lost their jobs.

35. If you are married with children and both you and your spouse work, see whose employer offers the best insurance deal. Don't buy duplicate coverage.

36. Find out if your insurance company practices capitation, the advance setting of fees per patient, and offers bonuses for minimizing costs.

37. Check your insurance plan for gag clauses that don't permit doctors to discuss alternative treatments not covered by the plan. There is too much potential for adverse risk under such conditions.

38. For increased use of tax deductibility, "bundle" as many qualifying medical expenses as possible within the same year to break through the 7.5 percent threshold required when itemizing deductions on IRS Schedule A.

39. If you would benefit more from using an employer's flexible spending account (FSA) for medical expenses, in which you can have money withheld from your paycheck before taxes, estimate how much you may incur during the year. Keep in mind that what you don't use is not refundable by the employer.

40. If you are an employer, your best bet may be a traditional indemnity (fee for service) contract that covers hospitalization

and major medical expenses. With a high deductible of several thousand dollars combined with a Medical Savings Account (same concept as the FSA), your employees could be well covered for much less than most health maintenance organization (HMO) or Preferred Provider Organization (PPO) plans.

41. Find out if your tap water is fluoridated and if not, give your children fluoride tablets as recommended by your dentist. Proper amounts of fluoride are well known to reduce the incidence of cavities by as much as 70 percent. According to Esther Wachs in the March, 1996, issue of *Forbes*, Americans received half as many fillings in 1990 as in 1959.

42. Get dental checkups and cleanings twice a year, especially for children, and get X rays less often than every year. There is a reluctance among many dentists to pass on dental records if you switch dentists, causing new dentists to order another full set of X rays, which are costly and of some health risk over time.

43. In addition to basic preventive dental care (daily flossing and brushing with a fluoride toothpaste), look into getting dental sealants for growing children, though beware that there is the possibility of sealing in decay as well.

44. Only buy dental insurance for the year(s) in which you and/or your family can bunch a lot of dental work together because over the long haul, you will pay far more for insurance premiums plus the percentage of dental costs not covered under most plans.

45. Stay buckled up all the time and remain fully alert while driving.

46. Take a first-aid and cardiopulmonary resuscitation (CPR) course to learn how to treat minor problems and certain emergencies that can't wait.

47. If you need copies of your medical records after hospitalization, your doctor may be able to get them to you for much less than the $1 to $2 per page cost that hospitals may charge.

48. If it is safe to do, drive yourself or have a friend drive you to the hospital instead of using an ambulance.

49. Consider using a certified nurse midwife to deliver your baby if your obstetrician has indicated you are at low risk.

50. Don't be misled by "miracle cures" such as vitamin megadosing, energy pills, and untested potions.

51. Beware of food product labeling. "All natural" does not always mean all good. "No preservatives" does not mean no artificial colors. However, "organic" is supposed to mean a food product

was raised without the use of pesticides or growth hormones, some of which may contain residual amounts of carcinogens.

52. Analyze your family history for three generations to help determine your risk of chronic diseases or conditions such as heart disease, diabetes, cancer, early menopause, etc.

53. If you don't have any of these risk factors and you're only in your 20s or 30s, pay for the least amount of health insurance you feel comfortable with. Keep in mind that paying more than a couple of hundred dollars a year for insurance may place you at a higher risk of financial hardship than incurring some outrageous medical bill.

54. Some employee insurance plans are very affordable. However, costs can increase greatly when including other family members in your plan. Weigh the benefits versus the costs of this insurance carefully.

55. Depending on the type of insurance you have, if you are healthy and low-risk, raise your deductible to substantially lower your premiums.

56. You and your doctor can petition or sue your insurance company if it won't pay for well-documented experimental treatments in potentially life-saving situations.

57. Check into fraternal, alumni, or trade organizations for group policies, if your employer doesn't cover you.

58. Be sure to get any discounts for not smoking or other lowered risks.

59. Don't buy insurance for specific risks such as cancer before checking to see if your regular insurance already covers these things.

60. Be sure your policy offers a stop-loss clause that ensures a ceiling on all out-of-pocket expenses beyond deductibles.

61. Skim your insurance policy to learn what is *not* covered, including all preexisting condition clauses. These days it can cost as much as $1,000 a month to buy individual coverage, which includes major preexisting conditions.

62. If you have a preexisting condition, sign up for coverage during an "open enrollment" period when all people are accepted regardless of condition.

63. Some doctors bill their work at rates higher than "usual and customary," which is what insurance companies pay. Ask your doctor to bill you at the rate your insurance company pays or

ask your insurance company to pay what the doctor charges
and stand firm.

64. Need more health care information? If you can't get enough
    from your local library, look into places such as Health Re-
    source, 501-329-5272, Planetree Health Information Service,
    415-923-3680, or The World Research Foundation, 818-907-
    5483, all of which provide comprehensive information about a
    variety of medical conditions for fees ranging from $45 to $250.
    Some computer on-line services, such as Medline, are helpful
    resources, as well.

65. Stay uninsured by choice through estimating your *perceived* risk
    against your *real* risk. This is a risk worth taking for those who
    are under the age of 40, have no serious high-risk factors in
    their family history, are in great health and work at remaining
    this way, don't engage in occupations that add significant risk
    factors, and can comfortably afford routine medical care and
    occasional office visits. If you do make this choice, are you dis-
    ciplined enough to take the money it would cost you and save
    or invest it?

66. Have you been persuaded that being uninsured is an act of ir-
    responsibility, causing taxpayers and those who are covered to
    bail you out? Being uninsured means that you are choosing *self-
    responsibility* by paying directly for your medical needs while,
    at the same time, placing downward cost pressure on the health
    care system. Insurance is a ticket for health care providers to
    charge more than what people can reasonably pay and perhaps
    the greatest barrier for many people in achieving their dreams.

67. If you earn a modest wage and obviously can't pay some med-
    ical bill that is several times your annual income, what is the an-
    swer? Laws vary from state to state, but perhaps the doctor/
    surgeon will take you as a charity case, known as indigent in
    health care terms, or take a modest sum of your savings and
    consider your bill paid. You also can try negotiating an interest-
    free payment plan through the hospital business office or per-
    haps you can negotiate a barter arrangement to work unpaid
    hours in the hospital. Even in a worst-case scenario, if you have
    legally concealed your assets and properly negotiated payment
    terms, you will not end up on the street corner with a cardboard
    sign, a fear insurance companies and the media have many
    people believing.

DISABILITY INSURANCE

There is a slight chance that because of some great misfortune you may become disabled at some time in your life and will incur substantial expenses and thus be forced to lose income from not working. Should you lose sleep worrying about the low risk of this possibility? No!

First of all, the chance of becoming disabled is even less likely in your younger years, when you are building your financial security, some of which can cushion such a setback. Also, if the cause of disability is definitely job-related, you ordinarily will be eligible for workers' compensation. In addition, your employer may provide you with limited coverage. Social Security also makes payments to the disabled, though the waiting period before benefits is five months. You can't collect full benefits from both simultaneously.

Under a variety of conditions you also have the right to sue to receive compensation, normally when you can prove you became disabled as a result of another's negligence. At the rate the court system takes, however, you could be left high and dry before receiving a windfall, and lawsuits don't come with guaranteed results.

So the question arises as to whether it is worth the expense to purchase private disability insurance. Estimate whether or not you might become disabled for a long enough duration to cut deeply into your savings and exceed the 30- to 90-day waiting periods of most policies. Don't forget to consider any family history you might have of suffering from long-term, disabling conditions. Then contemplate the outcomes of your safety nets, taking into account your spouse's income if there is any, and any comfortable downsizing you can implement. Factoring all this together probably will leave you questioning whether you need to buy disability coverage at all. Remember, people buy insurance for peace of mind, and this can be a good enough reason for many to spend money on it.

Disability policies can cost from around $1,800 to more than $5,000 a year, depending on the monthly benefit you want, your age, and health. Most workers in the 15 percent tax bracket can consider disability insurance a very low priority, usually skipping it altogether because it costs too great a percentage of one's income.

Typical coverage replaces 50 percent to 65 percent of a worker's income for a specified period of time such as three years, until age 65, or for life. Even if eligible for Social Security and workers' compensation, you still will not replace more than about 70 percent of your previous income and the percentage decreases as your earned income rises. Also keep in mind that benefits paid out by an employer or that you purchased with pretax dollars from an employer cafeteria plan are fully taxable, while benefits received from a private plan are tax-free.

Here are a few money-saving tips when buying long-term disability insurance:

- Determine exactly what your insurance covers. Some policies only pay under conditions of total disability, though some will pay full benefits for becoming blind or losing limbs, even if you still can continue to work.
- You also can buy such coverage just to ensure your ability to work in your occupation. To buy coverage for an extended period is considerably more expensive, though also that much more reassuring. A policy, for example, that pays $3,000 a month with a 90-day waiting period costs $2,150 a year, if payouts last a maximum of three years, and costs $2,900 a year if benefits last for life.
- Often waiting or elimination periods (the time before benefits begin) are 90 days, but by switching to 180 days you can save close to $400 on your policy. If you can live comfortably from other income sources for six months before needing the benefits, save the money. Going as low as 30 days is prohibitive in cost.
- Consider having guaranteed renewability built into your policy, so the company can't cancel your coverage and will guarantee fixed benefits, at a fixed premium.
- Also, look into buying inflation protection that increases benefit amounts to offset cost-of-living increases.
- Nonsmokers can receive up to a 25 percent discount.
- Those who pay their premium annually instead of monthly can pull down a slightly better rate.

The bottom line? Disability protection is very expensive and worth shopping around for inexpensive rates after determining your need. Note that a number of the guidelines for disability coverage resemble those for nursing-home insurance as well. Generally, when you take into account the limitations under which nursing-home insurance pays, how much it pays, alternatives that follow, your likelihood of being in a nursing home long-term, government safety nets, and implement wealth preservation strategies I discuss, you may feel that your premiums are insuring the profits of the insurance company more than your risk.

> ### Wisdom on Wealth
>
> Disability protection is very expensive and worth shopping around for inexpensive rates after determining your need.

HOME CARE

Having aging parents live in with their children will always be the most economical choice for long-term care, though far from the ideal or most practical solution in today's world. To offset some of the imposition this may cause, you might strike a deal in which your parents pay you a modest monthly income, which would be far less than a nursing home. If they are still reasonably independent, you may find that having them around is not so bad after all. I had a grandmother live in during my childhood who made a great baby-sitter for years until I had to baby-sit her. Incredible as this may sound, at today's nursing-home prices, the period of time she lived with my family would cost nearly a million dollars. Nursing homes do have their place, however. If your parents need round-the-clock attention, you may have to send them to a nursing home or hire full-time home nursing care, which also can be very costly (estimated from figures extrapolated from *Money* magazine, May, 1996, *Kiplinger's*, March, 1996, and *Smart Money*, December, 1995, to be up to $150,000 a year by 2010).

Having nursing or homemaking assistants come to your home *as needed* is much more economical than placing aging parents in nursing homes and permits your parents to remain in familiar surroundings. If all they need is someone to cook and clean for them, you can advertise locally to find someone who is reasonable and compatible. If your parents also require personal care such as bathing, dressing, etc., you will naturally want to be more selective. And if they require even more skilled care, a nurse may be necessary. At this point you might be able to contact home health care agencies through elderly resources in your area, though hiring a nurse directly may cost less. The Elder Care Locator, 800-677-1116, can be of assistance in starting this search.

Make sure the agency is licensed, accredited, and bonded. In addition, if it is Medicare-certified, the agency must meet certain federal standards. Find out what its services cost and to what extent it accepts

Medicare, Medicaid, or private insurance. Is there a 24-hour telephone line available? Can you establish a comfortable relationship between the agency and your parent's doctor? Will it send fully itemized bills? If the agency seems vague about financial concerns, go elsewhere. Some have been caught overbilling patients when they knew insurance would pay. Generally one should be able to hire as-needed care for $8,000 to $24,000 a year. The ideal situation might be to hire some trustworthy, compatible person and give him or her free room and board in exchange. This could save more than $12,000 a year! Also, consider relocating to an area where costs of nursing care are less. On the average, such care in Arizona, South Carolina, and Oregon can be a third less than in Florida, New York, and California.

MEDICARE/MEDIGAP

At this time all Americans are eligible for Medicare simply by reaching the age of 65. If you are of this age you can enroll by contacting your local Social Security office. There are two sections of Medicare: Part A, which covers a portion of hospital, skilled nursing, and hospice care; and Part B, which covers a percentage of medical needs such as doctor bills and certain medical supplies and equipment. Presently, there is no charge for Part A, because this is withheld from paychecks. Part B is optional and costs close to $50 a month (expected to rise to $90 by 2002), which is a great buy if you are without much private insurance. If you are in an HMO, so much the better—you may not need it. Medicare has a whole system of benefit periods, deductibles, coinsurance requirements, and other limitations that involve the patient paying a portion toward his or her care. Prescription drugs that can be very costly are not covered, though they may be covered through HMOs if you are fortunate enough to be enrolled in one. To get the most from your coverage be sure your doctor "accepts assignments," which assures that Medicare will pay 80 percent of the charges. Otherwise you will have to pay coinsurance plus 20 percent of the doctor's charges. Medicare will not pay the full 80 percent under certain conditions. You have the right to appeal, which although bureaucratic, can be successful. More than half the time people win their appeals, at least partially.

Medigap policies are purchased privately and are designed to cover what Medicare doesn't, which can add up to several thousand dollars a year. Federal law requires them to cover the 20 percent coinsurance and up to three pints of blood. Nine different types of plans cover a variety of services and prescription drugs, though some changes are being made. Understanding all this can become difficult and with the cost of such policies at more than $1,500 a year, you may not be getting value.

Never buy more than one Medigap policy, because you will be merely throwing money away. Be aware that it is illegal for an insurance company to sell you a policy if you already have one. One good law is that you can't be turned down for a preexisting condition if you apply for a Medigap policy within six months of becoming eligible for Medicare. Agents are to provide you with the *Guide to Health Insurance for People with Medicare*, published by the National Association of Insurance Commissioners and the Health Care Financing Administration. Read and understand it before writing a check. You have the right to cancel your policy within 30 days for a full refund. By the way, Medigap policies don't cover custodial care.

THE HOSPICE

Hospices are places where terminally ill people can choose to spend the last remaining weeks or months of their lives without any heroic medical intervention to prolong life. More than a million people have now used this far less costly alternative to hospitalization or nursing home care with a high degree of satisfaction. With about 2,500 hospices in the United States, no doubt there is one near you. If not, call the National Hospice Organization at 800-658-8898. Being admitted to a hospice is a decision you may reach after consulting with your doctor. If you want Medicare to pay, be sure the hospice is Medicare-certified.

INSURE YOUR WHEELS AFFORDABLY

Next to health insurance, automobile insurance is the most important insurance you can own. Throughout the United States, auto insurance is required to have a car on the road, with very few exceptions. Normally, only a minimum of liability coverage is required by state law, but depending on your individual circumstances, other aspects of car insurance may be highly recommended.

Price comparison is a necessity in saving money throughout this book and car insurance is no exception. The cost of insuring exactly the

---

Wisdom on Wealth

Price comparison is a necessity in saving money throughout this book and car insurance is no exception.

---

same vehicle for the same coverage in the same city can vary by as much as 60 percent, even for those with identical driving records. Automobile insurance isn't cheap anywhere, although it's less in areas with lower accident rates. Depending on numerous factors, insuring a car can cost from as little as $250 to more than $10,000 a year. According to the August, 1992, issue of *Consumer Reports,* the average household spent almost $9,000 combined insuring its vehicles over a period of ten years, yet filed only one claim for about $600 total during that same time period. You can lower your costs well below the nearly $1,000 yearly average by calling at least a dozen insurance companies after determining just what types of insurance coverage you want. Finding the lowest rates, however, should not be your only goal. You also want a highly rated company that provides decent service when you need it, responds politely and moves fast, pays appropriate claims, and does not easily cancel your policy just from one claim.

For better rates, try getting insurance from a "direct writer" that cuts costs by not paying sales commissions, which are typically around 15 percent. Some companies occasionally refund a portion of your premium later in the year if their claim payouts have been lower than estimated. I have used GEICO at 800-841-3000 for nearly 15 years and whenever I mention my rates, nobody I know seems to pay as little as I do. For California residents call 20th Century Insurance at 818-704-1487 or if you are or were an officer in the armed forces, call USAA at 800-531-8080. Of course, getting preferred rates is based on maintaining a great driving record, usually for three to five years or more.

HOW MUCH OF A RISK ARE YOU?

Some insurance companies tend to gear their services toward certain types of drivers. Whether drivers are young, old, safe, more accident-prone, or whatever, these factors can greatly affect your rates. When determining how much to charge or even whether to accept you at all, insurers take into account factors other than your age and driving record. Some of the most important ones are gender, the number of miles you drive each year, where you live, your marital status, and if you are a smoker and/or drinker. You can expect to pay far more for your insurance if you live in a city than the suburbs or a rural area. Even a history of job instability, poor credit, quality of academic performance, or out-of-the-ordinary working hours can affect your policy. If you should be caught lying on your insurance application, the insurance company has the right to decline coverage.

For those who are in the very high-risk category, such as those who have had several accidents, are very young, or new to the country, nonstandard policies are available from some insurance companies and state insurance pools. The premiums, however, are so high ($1,000 to more than $3,000 a year) that it becomes highly questionable as to whether it is worth spending this much money just for driving privileges.

COLLISION AND COMPREHENSIVE

If you expect to pay for collision coverage, you must realize that this is quite an expensive option. Collision covers the cost of accident-related repairs or replacement of your vehicle. It normally comes with a deductible as low as $100, which means you pay the first $100 toward repairs that are your fault, unless you live in a no-fault state. Of course, the higher the value of your vehicle, the costlier this coverage is, though the safety rating of the vehicle is also taken into account. Collision costs are more on a new car, too. As a car ages, its value goes down, and beyond a few years, it no longer is worth having collision protection. A common rule of thumb is to drop collision coverage when the premium equals 10 percent of the value of the car. Here are a few more money-saving tips for paying car insurance:

- One major step you can take to lower the cost of premiums is to raise the deductible. Depending on the make and model of your car, raising the deductible from under $500 to at least $1,000 could save you from $50 to more than $200 a year. It is never worth having low collision deductibles because, even though you save money toward repairs, after an accident you immediately become a high-risk driver and pay higher insurance premiums.
- To avoid high rates after an accident, don't file claims of under $1,000 with your insurance company. In fact, when in an accident

caused by you, with minor damage to the other vehicle, try to negotiate to pay the other driver yourself for repairs to his or her car. This may cost you less than having your insurance company "black list" you as a bad driver. If you cause another accident within three years, your premiums may shoot through the roof. And if you have a third accident, you may have to find another insurance company or resort to a state insurance pool, which is very expensive. So buy the $1,000 or more deductible coverage and pay for the fender-benders yourself. Also, be alert to the fact that some insurance companies have a "first accident allowance" in which drivers with established clean records may not be surcharged for their first at-fault accident.

- Should you not have been involved in any accidents yet suspect your insurance rates seem too high, your computerized Comprehensive Loss Underwriting Exchange (CLUE) could contain misinformation. Call Equifax, 800-456-6004 to inquire about your CLUE record.
- For young adults under the age of 21, the cost of car insurance may be prohibitive because people this young, especially males, are statistically in a high-risk category. Rates get better after the age of 21 and much better in most states at age 25, assuming one has maintained a clean and accident-free driving record.
- Young adults under the age of 25 should be encouraged to not register their car in their own names, even if they are responsible drivers. Parents can register cars with their children on their policy for much less than young adults can under their own policy. Or if a young adult marries someone over the age threshold, he or she could save money by keeping the car insured under the older person's policy.
- Your comprehensive coverage takes care of damage to your car from events not caused by accidents, such as theft, vandalism, fire, storm damage, and riots. As with collision coverage, as a car depreciates in value, comprehensive coverage, which is optional, becomes less important. Drop it when its cost equals 10 percent of the value of the vehicle.
- Comprehensive coverage will cost less if you keep your car in a safe place at night, such as in your locked garage, avoid high crime areas when you park, do not leave expensive stereo systems or other costly items in plain view, and have a steering wheel lock and/or alarm system installed. In fact, with all of

these precautions, you may be able to get by without any comprehensive protection unless your car has a very high resale value.

- If a vehicle is off the road, for whatever reason, for more than a month and you can easily prove it, the insurance company may prorate your premium accordingly. This applies for other people on the policy, such as children who are at college for many months at a time. You should not have to pay the extra fee if you can show that they are not using your car for an extended period. In some states, you may be required to relinquish your license plates to fully prove that the car is off the road.

- You can contact your insurance company to find out how your premium costs are affected by traffic tickets. Some will not adjust your policy for just one ticket and may not for two. Some send out questionnaires asking you to report your tickets and then either cross-reference them with public safety records or at least spot-check. If you are caught with outstanding tickets that you did not report, your insurance company has the right to make you pay the difference of higher premium costs retroactively and will immediately adjust your present costs. Parking tickets do not count against your insurance, only moving violations do.

- Try to avoid paying for automobile insurance by the month, for it will cost more because of service charges. If you have more than one vehicle in the family, place all of them on one policy and save money on processing fees.

- Be sure to let your insurance company know if you took a defensive driving course, have automatic safety belts, air bags, antilock brakes, or antitheft devices. You might qualify for additional savings on your premium.

- Find out if your insurance company offers other forms of insurance such as homeowners', renters', boat, health, life, etc. Many offer a further discount for handling all your insurance business. Of course, if some of the other rates are not competitive, this strategy may not be sensible.

- Don't bother to get emergency-road-service protection because on the average it will not pay off. For the approximately $18 a year, you would need to be towed every three years just to break even. How many times have you been towed in your years of driving?

- As to how much protection to buy in general, consider how much you drive, where you drive, your economic status (how high a risk you can handle), your driving record, what other drivers use your car under the policy and their driving record, the make of your car, and its value.

- Uninsured motorist insurance, which is mandatory in some states, insures the driver, other passengers in the car, and family members in the event that a collision occurs with an uninsured or hit-and-run driver. It consists of additional liability protection. Usually, it is unnecessary because regular liability coverage already covers the driver and passengers regardless of whether a collision takes place with an insured or uninsured driver, hit-and-run driver, or a tree. In fact, most policies say "Any amount otherwise payable for damages under uninsured motorists shall be reduced by any sum paid under the liability coverage of this policy," significantly limiting its value. On the average, when it does pay, the amount of this coverage is less than the added cost over a several-year period. Also, most policies will only pay what workers' compensation or other benefits don't.
- Underinsured-motorist protection pays for expenses beyond the amount of the other driver's insurance. If one incurs $80,000 of damages and medical bills from an accident and the other person who caused the crash only carried $50,000 of protection, for example, then the uninsured coverage would pay the other $30,000 minus the policy's deductible. Uninsured and underinsured protection only adds about $20 to $40 a year to most policies so consider eliminating this slight risk for this modest sum.
- Personal injury protection (PIP) is a broad medical coverage offered in states with no-fault insurance. PIP goes well beyond merely medical payments—reimbursing for some funeral bills, paying for certain lost wages, and essential services to the insured. If this coverage significantly overlaps existing disability insurance, then money is being wasted. Never buy duplicate coverage because only one policy will pay you.

HOMEOWNER'S INSURANCE

Finally, we come to homeowner's insurance. How much hazard insurance should you buy for your home? As with all insurance, the true bottom line lies in how much risk you are willing to take. Generally, insurance experts recommend using the 80 percent rule in which coverage equals at least 80 percent of the cost to rebuild your home. For a higher premium, you can shift the burden of determining the value of your home to the insurance company, which will set your policy with a replacement cost guarantee. This type of policy will cover the full cost of replacement even if the cost is more than the amount of your insurance. Full replacement cost of all the contents is available as well. While replacement cost guarantees provide peace of mind, the risk of needing this option is very low and probably not worth the extra cost.

You can reduce risk yourself by making wise choices, such as not purchasing a home on a floodplain, or in an earthquake, hurricane, or crime-prone area, and taking common-sense precautions with potential fire hazards. Proper storage of flammable materials, safe use of electrical and gas appliances, keeping your furnace in working order, and installing a couple of smoke detectors normally reduces fire risk to practically zero. As for insuring specific valuables such as expensive jewelry, you can purchase riders on your policy just for this purpose. If these items are worth more than a couple of thousand dollars, either sell them and invest the cash or hide them in obscure places, such as in attic insulation far from the attic door, so that any burglar would have to spend more time than it's worth to find them. Just don't forget where you hide such things!

Is a home-security system worth the few hundred dollars' investment plus the $20 to $30 monthly fees? The 15 percent you save off of your insurance (only on alarms that dial the police) comes short of offsetting the cost of the system. Also, my research has indicated that security systems fail to do their jobs most of the time, and cities have so many false-alarm problems that they now charge false alarm fines. In Seattle, there were fewer than 30 arrests out of 5,600 break-ins reported in recent years, so I question their value even more. Worst of all, most burglars know that once the alarm goes off they normally have about ten minutes before the police will come. Ten minutes can cost you a fortune.

The worst hazard you may have to worry about is when your hazard insurance won't cover a hazard. It is common for insurance companies to drop people's insurance altogether after they have made claims once or twice. Of course, this practice is grossly unfair to the homeowner who has suffered through two roof-destroying hailstorms within a year or two. Insurers are resisting state pressure to divulge their underwriting guidelines at the time of this writing, claiming these are trade secrets. It's long overdue for all to have access to this information. If your insurance company does try to drop your coverage, first try appealing through your agent. If you lose the battle, then call around to other companies and your state insurance department, who may have insurance pools you can join at a higher cost.

Estimating how much insurance to buy is simple in one way, based on the assumption of a risk being insignificantly low and, therefore, not worth insuring. On the other hand if you are the one who must confront a calamity, it may be like winning the lottery *in reverse*. I realize that I recommend being more of a risk taker than average (while taking an active role in reducing risk yourself) and I continue to adhere to this philosophy, not only because it has permitted me to improve my financial status considerably but statistically can do the same for you. For the few who end up with the reverse-lottery winning, insurance is not always the answer. In fact, insurance is much of the root cause of catastrophic medical problems, accidents, funeral and burial costs, etc., being so overpriced. For example, it is common sense that as long as millions of people can simply show their HMO card to permit nearly endless billing, health care costs will not come down. Also, insurance can be a disincentive toward self-responsibility.

The bottom line is:

- Keep your lifestyle low-risk and preventively oriented.
- Invest the money you save on insurance in profitable and financially stable investments.
- Be aware that spending money on heavy insurance coverage can cost you several thousand dollars a year while only reducing financial risk in your life by a small percentage.
- Keep in mind that in most cases it costs less to pay off a debt from an uninsured mishap over time than to maintain an everlasting "debt" to insurance companies.
- When you buy insurance, get high deductibles to insure only the worst catastrophies.

Whether to purchase insurance, what type, and how much is not an easy choice in many cases. Numerous risk factors are tied largely to your individual circumstances, which means *only you* can ultimately make the final determination. What I hope this chapter has done is to raise your objectivity toward the topic because spending on insurance is often a response to an emotional need or fear rather than reality. In addition, you may have come to realize how much money you can save by exerting your own risk controls through living a more healthy and responsible life.

CHAPTER 8

Slashing Your Utility Bills

Now let's look at where you can save lots of money in the use of energy and water. Automobile use, heat and air-conditioning, lights, appliances, the use of recyclable materials, the efficient use of water, and the wise use of the telephone are all areas where considerable savings can be found. The real challenge in conserving resources is doing so while continuing to maintain a satisfying lifestyle. In other words, can you use less while not giving up something? I believe you can actually have a *better* lifestyle through using less as you will see! As referred to earlier, accomplishing the same tasks with less resources frees up those resources to expand the capacity of your life.

Wisdom on Wealth

The real challenge in conserving resources is doing so while continuing to maintain a satisfying lifestyle.

TRANSPORTATION

Consider the following cost-saving measures while reevaluating your transportation needs:

- Public transportation quickly translates into major savings in gasoline, vehicle maintenance, and insurance costs. So when purchasing your next vehicle, make *fuel economy* a major consideration.
- Combine trips.
- Use air-conditioning only when you can't get comfortable by rolling down the windows because air-conditioning consumes more fuel.
- Avoid sudden starts and coast with your foot off the gas well ahead of necessary stops.
- Live close to work and other conveniences for which the car is needed. Doing so saves thousands of miles of car use a year, which not only saves gas but also extends the life of your vehicle and reduces repairs—let alone time.
- If moving near your workplace is out of the question for well-founded practical reasons, try carpooling with coworkers.
- Consider the feasibility of walking or riding a bicycle that can provide health benefits as well as save gas and car use.
- Determine if your household can reduce the number of cars in its possession.
- Unless your car is a tank-size gas guzzler and/or seriously depleting your bank account in repairs, keep it in top running condition and drive it until it dies. I normally operate with the philosophy of making full use of expensive, durable items such as houses, cars, and appliances—maintaining them for the long-term, because regularly moving or replacing things multiplies their cost considerably. (You can apply this principle right on down to small items as well. Just how small is up to you. I have used the same paper bag for my lunch for a month before it would no longer hold a sandwich and piece of fruit while others threw theirs in the trash each day or have cut papers towels in half to get twice the use from the roll. However, in doing so I also have realized that, while such habits are environmentally friendly, the actual amount of money saved is simply not worth mentioning.)

Wisdom on Wealth

The bottom line here is little more than common sense. Whether you use electricity, gas, or oil, the more you use, the more it costs.

INSIDE YOUR HOME

Can you use less and still be comfortable? You bet! A wealth of savings in energy consumption is possible inside the home. Merely wearing a wool sweater (even at the $100 full price, you will recoup your investment fast) in the winter and setting the thermostat at 65 degrees and less while sleeping and at work, and dressing light and setting it to near 80 degrees in the summer will lower your utility bill significantly. Generally, for each degree you set the thermostat up in the summer, you trim 5 percent off your cooling bill, while saving closer to 2 percent for each degree lowered in the winter. Of course, properly insulating—plugging up cracks around windows, doors, electric sockets, chimney flues (when ready to use the fireplace, don't forget to be sure the flue is properly ventilating) and air-conditioning/heating vents and ductwork—can add to the efficient use of energy as well. The efficient and frequent maintenance of furnaces and air-conditioning systems is also essential for maximum benefit. Simply placing your air-conditioning unit in the shade can save another 5 percent on electricity. If you own your home, check out your level of attic insulation and its R-factor, which is the energy efficiency rating. Ideally, most homes should have at least a foot of cellulose or fiberglass insulation throughout the attic, with around 16 inches being the maximum in cost efficiency for energy saved. A single conventional pane of window glass is hardly over R-1, while 16 inches of fiberglass is R-49. In some areas utility companies cover the cost of upgrading homes in energy efficiency or at least supply information and advice on what your home needs, for even though they are in the business of selling power, delaying the cost of building more power plants saves them money. Others offer rebates and low-interest loans for purchasing energy-conserving equipment and materials. Consumers can often get a break on usage rates during off-peak hours. By far the largest factor in energy consumption is the *climate* you live in as well as the local utility rates.

THE PURCHASE AND USE OF MAJOR APPLIANCES

More efficient appliances are on the market now, which is good, but unfortunately many of them are more expensive and in some cases not worth their extra cost. The more you use a highly efficient appliance, the more savings you gain over using a less efficient one to perform the same task. But if the "same task" is to heat or cool a home to a comfort level that could be reached through other methods that involve not running the machine at all for longer periods, then weigh and balance the savings in greater efficiency. If you have been operating an air-conditioning unit for 20 hours a week at a cost of $60 a month and the new efficient model costs $45 a month to operate under the same conditions, for example, you will save about $85 during a typical summer in Austin, Texas. If you demand 24-hour comfort, however, your savings could approach $500. Considering that most people shut off the machine or leave the thermostat set higher when out a number of hours each week while working, etc., an average savings may come to around $275 during the cooling season. If you are extremely thrifty and only run it for a little while before bedtime each day, you can keep your old, less-efficient system a while longer because your savings may be only around $50 a summer. In this case it is penny-wise to delay the several-thousand-dollar purchase of a new system. Another alternative with air-conditioning is to purchase a window unit or two, especially for homes in the North where the cooling season is relatively brief.

THE SEASONAL ENERGY EFFICIENCY RATIO (SEER) AND COSTS

Heating and air-conditioning systems all have a Seasonal Energy Efficiency Ratio (SEER) rating number and/or Annual Fuel Utilization Efficiencies (AFUE) rating, measured in percentage terms of how effectively fuel is converted to heat, the higher representing greater efficiency, at least in theory. An air conditioner with a SEER of 7 will cost more to operate than one with a rating of 10. One rated at 16, however, will not save much over the 10 and may actually be less economical, according to an air-conditioning and heating engineer I know. Also, the 16 SEER machine will have a much higher purchase price than the 10 and over a few years its efficiency may decrease anyway. Also understand that furnaces and air-conditioning systems must be properly matched to the area they are warming or cooling. If you own an all-electric home and can't change over to gas heat, look into electric heat pumps that can save up to 25 percent on power use, especially in warmer climates.

WHERE TO BUY IT

Finding honest people in the industry is not easy. I have been informed by a couple of honest sales and service technicians that it is estimated that close to 80 percent of businesses in the air-conditioning and heating industry in central Texas are not properly informing customers on what they need and are overcharging for new equipment. Try shopping around and getting referrals from friends and neighbors. I have found the honest service people to be those in business for themselves and whose little overhead and advertising costs let them offer better rates. If they can't explain how systems operate, SEER/AFUE ratings and just what they mean, and take an active interest in the size of your home and lifestyle as it relates to heating and cooling needs, then you can assume they are more interested in a sales commission and probably have little training. When I had my system replaced, I received estimates as high as $4,700 but ended up getting much better service for $2,000.

THE HOT WATER HEATER CAN CHILL
YOUR BANK ACCOUNT

Shading windows that face the sun in the summer and letting in the sun during the winter can help some (consider the path to the sun relative to the orientation of a home you are thinking of buying), but lowering the temperature on your hot-water heater creates immediate, year-round savings. Most are factory-set at 140 to 160 degrees, which is intolerably hot and downright dangerous. Lower the temperature to your personal comfort level. My household has plenty of hot water with the thermostat set at 115 to 120 degrees and saves at least $10 a month over leaving it factory-set. When you must consistently mix cold water with hot to bathe, then the temperature is hotter than necessary. You can add further to this savings by purchasing a timer that can be set to switch on and off only during the times when you need hot water. Intermatic makes several versions from $20 to $40 that can be programmed with various settings (available at your local home supply center). Some may argue that the hot-water heater has to work so hard to heat up the water after many hours of being off that it does not save much, but my timer was paid for within two to three months in electric savings. If you will be leaving home for an extended period of time, shut off the hot-water heater, though not if there is any risk of pipes freezing. Tankless water heaters now are on the market that fit under sinks. The advantages of these units are getting hot water almost instantly, which saves time, water, and space for having a tank; but for a family that takes three showers and has the dishwasher running all within a short period, forget it. To avoid wasting water while waiting for it to get warm, simply fill an empty milk jug with cold water first and use it to water the garden or chill it for drinking.

Wisdom on Wealth

Generally, appliances that heat up such as ovens, dishwashers, space heaters, and clothes dryers use more power. Gas is the most economical to heat with, oil comes in second, and electric is the most costly.

OTHER ENERGY USE COMPARISONS

Computers, TVs, VCRs, lights, radios, clocks, and compact disc players use comparatively little energy. Refrigerators use a modest amount of power to do their job and can be kept efficient simply by cleaning dust off the coils on the back that restrict the flow of heat out and making sure all seals around the doors remain tight. Fluorescent lights use much less power for the same amount of light output, and microwave ovens heat food far more efficiently than conventional ovens. The compact fluorescent lights are available as 5 watts equaling the brightness of a 25-watt bulb, 7 watts equaling a 40-watt bulb, 11 watts equaling a 75-watt bulb, and 15 watts putting out the brightness of a standard 100-watt lamp. Though fluorescent bulbs are quite costly, they will save considerably over their long life, which can be as much as ten times the life of an ordinary bulb, plus provide the added benefit of generating less heat, which saves on air-conditioning costs. The new Halogen bulbs also are a good cost-saving bright alternative. These alternative lights are especially economical if used for lighting several hours or more daily such as for outdoor security lighting.

Operating an average-size room, window, or ceiling fan uses about 40 times less power, about as much as a 60- to 75-watt lightbulb, as a window air conditioner, or close to 75 times less than a central air-conditioning system. At least for your own amusement go look at your electric meter and watch how fast the rotating disk spins as you switch on and off a variety of appliances, lights, and other things that use electricity. The faster it goes, the thinner your wallet becomes.

DON'T GET SOAKED BY YOUR WATER BILL

If you have a swimming pool, this will most likely be the largest user of water. Some may wish to let it dry out for fear that they will drown in their water bill and, therefore, never achieve financial independence. Hopefully, most will simply expect higher water bills. In some communities residents may obtain a permit from their town for only $20 to $30 to fill their pools from a fire hydrant, which should be a savings over filling it from the tap and probably faster, too. Careful consideration also should go into the decision to own a pool because in addition to the enormous quantity of water it uses, there are also maintenance costs such as repairs of occasional leaks from cracking, addition of chemicals, keeping debris out, and electricity to heat it if it is so equipped. Pools are great in hot climates but consider how convenient it is versus using a nearby public pool.

The next largest user of water is the toilet, which, in most older homes, uses close to five gallons per flush. Depending on the size of your household, water consumption from toilet use could exceed that used in a year for a swimming pool. Conceivably, a typical family of four could generate about 12 flushes a day, equaling 60 gallons, 1,800 gallons a month, or nearly 22,000 gallons a year. There are only three strategies for reducing this consumption, the last of which I don't generally recommend for obvious reasons. One is to purchase a new toilet that uses only 1.5 gallons per flush, priced from under $75 to $250 in home-supply stores (installation may cost another $100 or so unless you install it yourself). One obvious disadvantage is that for this initial cost, you could buy a lot of city water. Another I have discovered is the fact that the water level is so low in most of them that frequently two flushes are required after use plus more frequent cleaning is needed. A second method is to place an object in the tank, such as a plastic milk jug, which displaces water with each flush. And no, you don't need to go by a third method advised by former mayor Ed Koch of New York a number of years ago during a critical water shortage, "When it's brown, flush it down, but stay mellow when it's yellow."

Keeping the water pressure low and staying in the shower for shorter periods of time adds further to water savings, as does running dishwashers and washing machines only when they are full. I have not found much value in installing low-flow shower-heads because merely lowering the pressure has the same effect. The debate over whether it uses more water to wash dishes by hand or using a dish-washer lingers on. I figure that when one takes into account the cost of a dishwasher, its maintenance, and the time it takes to load and unload the machine, one may break even. The lawn sprinkler is another major consumer of water. Avoid watering when the sun is up to reduce evap-oration. Planting grasses and shrubs that are drought-tolerant in hot climates (known as xeriscaping) can also reduce consumption consid-erably. And last of all, repair any leaks, no matter how small, as soon as possible.

Good equipment for the collection of rain water is just beginning to enter the market but it is not yet worth the cost in most cases. If you have access to large, durable containers, try directing the flow of down-spouts into them and install a standard-size outdoor water faucet near their bottoms to gravity-feed water into a hose for lawn and garden use. I have a couple of 55-gallon heavy plastic barrels I purchased for just $15 each that work perfectly and provide me with 110 free gallons with each rain. Also, where I live it is common practice for people to pipe out the water outflow from their washing machines to water their yard (most biodegradable detergents seem to act as fertilizers for lawns and gardens). Also regarding washing machines, front-loading washers use a third less water and energy than top loaders though they don't seem very popular in stores. Innovators have provided hot water in their homes by using a hose spiraling down their hot roofs in the summer into holding tanks, while others have developed ways of using solar and wind power for a variety of applications. Unfortunately, alternative methods of harnessing our natural resources are still not yet engineered on a mass-production scale.

RECORD YOUR CONSUMPTION

Here is a sample of the type of chart I have used to realize how much utility usage changes throughout the year:

Utility Usage Chart

Year/Month	KW Hours	Cost	Units/ Water	Cost	Comments
1996 Jan.	534	29.67	3,250	9.85	heat 12 days
Feb.	497	28.16	3,325	8.57	heat 8 days

Try maintaining a chart of this type for a full year—seasonal changes can be quite significant. Under the comment column you can refer to the frequency you had to water your garden, how extra hot or cold it was, or how much rain you had during a month and if you replaced or added a new appliance. You can alter your use patterns and make adjustments to your thermostat and watch the differences in cost by the month. Because my home is all-electric, I only show columns for electricity and water. You can design your own chart to accommodate oil or gas consumption.

Because of major differences in climate and other factors, the cost per unit of fuel and water varies widely throughout the country. Utility costs, however, do not necessarily reflect overall costs of living. For example, I moved from suburban Boston to Austin a number of years ago. In the Boston suburb one could run a lawn sprinkler as often as he or she wished and not worry about the water bill exceeding $5 a month, while the equivalent amount of water in Austin costs $45 a month. Based on this alone, naturally one would choose Boston. But the same-size home in the Boston suburb I moved from that we own in Austin would cost more than double in the Boston area with higher property taxes as well.

TV—IS IT WORTH IT?

How much and what type of television you watch is your choice as an individual. The purchase of a TV will not set most people back much with color sets now costing as little as $125 and VCRs for not much more than this. But paying for cable TV can range anywhere from about $20 to $70 month, depending on the number of channels you want, how often you watch pay-per-view movies, or if you rent satellite equipment. Though the reception, variety, and programming quality of some shows is a great improvement over standard VHF and UHF, analyze how much of what your household watches or needs. And shop around among standard cable, wireless cable, and satellite, and check out what telephone companies are now offering. Some are providing Internet access as well, which may be more competitive than most of the present on-line services. Also, private Internet access providers charge as little as $99 a year for practically unlimited service. The best Internet deals are for those that are associated with various institutions such as universities, school districts, and large corporations that charge a one-time or annual modest fee of under $10 for unlimited access.

DON'T SPEND A FORTUNE TO TALK

Telephone service is another area in which you can find plenty of savings. It is truly amazing to be able to talk to anyone, anytime, and anywhere on the planet who has another telephone! The telephone has created as much change in our society as any other invention, with people who are close being able to instantly communicate. The prices of all types of telephones from wired to cordless and cellular have dropped considerably, along with some of the rates for their use. I believe that it is worth investing in quality telephone equipment because it just isn't worth the aggravation of having trouble getting through or hearing someone. The new digital cellulars are truly superb in sound quality. And the competition among cellular companies is more fierce than ever lately, with many generous promotions being offered.

Dealing with telephone companies offers many saving opportunities. In most parts of the country local service providers charge from $50 to $75 to start telephone service. If the prior residents at the location into which you are moving had their telephone service disconnected, this fee is unavoidable unless you can prove your income is below a certain threshold, normally government poverty guidelines, in which case you can be eligible for such programs as Southwestern Bell's "Link Up America" program, no doubt offered by other local telephone companies. If you can meet the resident of the dwelling you are moving into, try asking him or her to leave the telephone connected, which can save you the switch-on fee, because all the telephone company has to change is the name on the computer record rather than disconnect and reconnect service. There may be a nominal fee for changing the name. You must work out this arrangement responsibly with the previous resident in terms of when this billing name change takes place, after which you are the person to be billed. An option that people rarely exercise is to request a party line, which can cut your local monthly charge by as much as 50 percent. Having a party line may not be convenient to most people because it means sharing your telephone with someone else, such as a neighbor, but for those who are not telephone junkies, $100 or so a year savings may be worth it. Also, keep in mind that the area of the country in which you have a telephone has major effects on the local rates. I have a friend in Maryland who pays under $8 a month for basic service, while it cost me $23 out in New Mexico once, the excuse given by Mountain Bell was that the cost of planting lines over long distances in the West cost more.

Tailor your telephone services to suit your needs. Some telephone companies offer measured service, which provides you with a limited number of free local calls each month, after which you will be billed from 5 to 20 cents each for additional calls. Another option in some areas is to base the cost of each call you make on how long you chat, just as long-distance calls are, though nowhere near this expensive. Obviously for those who talk at length or make lots of calls, it works out better to have unlimited local service. Most suburban areas offer extended range calling, in which you can call a broader area on an unlimited basis for a few extra dollars per month. One fee that is a slow leak on the bank accounts of several million Americans is a telephone rental fee that goes back many years when the Bell System had a monopoly on telephone service. This several-dollar-a-month charge is *entirely needless* because anyone can go buy a telephone for well under $20 and give AT&T their telephone back, which he or she has probably paid for many times in rental costs.

Numerous optional extras can cost from nothing to a couple of dollars a month. Most do have an added monthly charge of $1.50 to $7 and, therefore, should be subscribed to only if the amount of time and/or money saved from these services is actually worth their cost. The services I am referring to are such options as Call Waiting, Call Return, Call Forwarding, Caller ID, Voice Mail, Redial, and others. Local service can easily triple depending on how many of these extras you request. Estimate the value of such services versus their cost.

Even though Touch-Tone service seems quite standard these days, it also costs extra each month, so unless you make so many calls that the few seconds of time saved by having Touch-Tone is of measurable value, keep your old rotary telephones or buy the type that has the tone or pulse option switch that permits button pushing for dialing and can still access the many Touch-Tone automated answering systems. This can be done simply by switching from pulse to tone once the call has gone through. When arranging new service, telephone company representatives will try to talk you into paying another $2 or so monthly for potential home wiring problems with the threat that if you experience such troubles, it will cost more than $150 an hour to have a service technician come out and do the needed work. Except in ancient homes, telephone wiring almost never fails, and when it does, most jobs are simple to do without the help of a technician.

LONG-DISTANCE CALLING

As we all know, the competition among long-distance providers has become fierce in recent times. Though the big three, AT&T, MCI, and Sprint, make themselves obvious to us through their constant, massive advertising and telemarketing campaigns, many hundreds of smaller companies are actually in this business, some of which are even more competitive. I will not attempt to compare rates, promotions, bonuses, and calling plans among different companies here because it could nearly fill another book and it would be outdated long before it could be printed and distributed. For those who do make large amounts of long-distance calls, I recommend they invest $12.95 to order the latest *Long Distance Resellers Source Book*, published every spring and fall by *Phone+ Magazine* at 602-990-1101, which makes an honest crack at keeping up. Incentives to sign up can involve air miles, free calling time, gift certificates, magazine subscriptions, discount calling plans, free pager use for a time period, and cash bonuses. Some people switch often enough to get enough cash incentives to end up averaging no cost for their telephones at all, a perfectly legal maneuver. Generally, with most companies it is still much cheaper to call on weekends, holidays, or between 11 PM and 8 AM, with evening rates priced higher, and weekday time rates per minute the highest. More and more local and long-distance providers are entering each other's territory, which is inviting even more competition, so prices should continue to be very competitive. A real convenience available through using telephone code numbers is being able to access a variety of long-distance companies at the same time. In other words, for example, if MCI has a better weekend rate than AT&T does, you can access MCI by using a code even though you have AT&T as your main long-distance carrier, or you can use Sprint to obtain a better weekday rate. Your telephone bill may show several companies listed at the end of the month, but if you have saved money, that's what counts! Also, consider getting a personal incoming 800 number that could be ideal for family members who must be away from home for a while. What you really must be extra careful of is using public telephones and calling cards. "Operator service providers" have jurisdiction over quite a number of public telephones now, many of which are charging outrageous rates. Some people may be receiving bills for as much as $5 to $12 for a one-minute call within the United States, while any of the big three would charge from under a dollar to about $1.50. And many of these telephones will not let you access your carrier or use your calling card. Also some calling cards, even among the big three, vary in service charges considerably, so if you plan to make regular use of calling cards, inquire about their rates when switching companies. For households in which there is a frequent need for calling home from far away, it may be more economical to have a personal 800 number that eliminates the need for a calling card. With such heavy competition, you have some bargaining power, though nothing will save as much as simply spending less time on the telephone, or using cheaper alternatives such as e-mail or fax.

CHAPTER 9

Cashing in on Life's Freebies, Bargains, and Pleasures

This chapter is about getting the most mileage from your dollar. Not a week passes that I don't receive offers to keep on borrowing money and incentives to keep spending it. If it isn't an offer for another preapproved credit card, it's an offer for a several-thousand-dollar loan from some finance company. Travel clubs, free trial memberships, buy-one-get-one-free offers, book and CD club deals, get-rich-quick manuals (which only pad the pockets of their authors), and an endless variety of insurance offers come knocking at our door constantly. The telephone rings trying to get us to have our carpet cleaned, purchase life insurance, switch our long-distance service, or subscribe to a newspaper. Then the doorbell rings with an innocent eight-year-old selling candy bars for $1.25 to raise funds for the school band trip. I have had solicitation by mail, telephone, and my front door within the same hour a couple of times!

Can you manage to say no and keep your wallet closed through all of this? Maybe not all the time. Just choose selectively, make purchases count, and avoid making unplanned purchases for things that may end up in your local thrift store within the year. In nearly every direction you look, business is trying to get a piece of what you have worked so hard to get: *your money*.

Are all these money-saving offers truly worthwhile? Coupons are great to use when they are for products or services you need to make

---

Wisdom on Wealth

In nearly every direction you look, business is trying to get a piece of what you have worked so hard to get: *your money.*

---

use of anyway. Travel clubs do provide much useful information, 95 percent of which is available in your local public library. I would say 100 percent, except that some information in the library may be a little out-of-date. Some travel clubs offer free traveler's checks and some other travel discounts as well.

Free trial memberships are fine as long as you understand the rules. You will indeed get a sizable collection of very low-cost books, compact discs, toys, or whatever a club is offering. However, you will be expected to purchase a substantial quantity of other goods at the "regular price" for a certain period of time. This regular price may be discounted somewhat, but is still more than you may wish to spend. As for get-rich manuals and life insurance sold by mail, they can do little more than drain your bank account to fill someone else's.

DON'T DRIVE YOURSELF INTO DEBT

Because people *spend* a fortune over their lifetimes on personal transportation, here is how you can *save* a fortune:

- Don't buy a car brand new unless you are in a very comfortable position to do so. The second a new vehicle is driven off the dealer's lot, it depreciates in value by several thousand dollars. For those who are fortunate enough to pay cash for a new car, yet naturally want the best deal, do your research and bargain hard. Go to your library or bookstore and find out your dealer's cost, which will tell you the bargaining room you have.
- Dealers want to sell cars badly enough at times to offer some better deals. One factor to consider is the day supply of unsold cars that fluctuates monthly. When cars have been sitting on dealer lots more than 75 to 100 days, factory and dealer incentives such as rebates, accessories at no extra charge, and better financing rates (sometimes under 5 percent) are promoted. You can get this information faxed to you for $10 from the Crain Information Cen-

ter (313-446-0367). For foreign vehicles built in the United States, call Ward's Automotive Reports, 810-357-0800. This information is less available for cars built outside the United States.

- Dealers are paying manufacturer's interest each month for vehicles to sit on their lot, so buying at the end of the month can place you in a better position to bargain as well as at the end of a day, when dealers are anxious to close up.
- Buying off the lot is naturally preferred by dealers than special ordering, so if you are not too choosy about color and options, you may get a better deal.
- Consider how important extras are beyond air-conditioning, a basic sound system, and power brakes, because they can add on more than $1,000 to the basic price.
- Try to avoid financing cars if possible because you will pay far more for the vehicle over time and have to carry full insurance coverage until loans are paid. Sadly, many people are trapped into monthly payments because by the time they pay up, they are out buying another car again. These constant debt payments can keep you from ever getting ahead.
- If you can, use public transportation, carpool, or bicycle.
- If you do use financing, don't buy the credit life insurance that pays off the loan if you die. It is overpriced and the finance company can repossess the car to pay it off in case of death anyway.
- Buying a good used car with modest mileage is your best bet. I have found that buying a used car through newspaper classified ads is the best bargain, though you risk full liability if your car breaks down, unlike the limited warranty some dealers can provide.
- Lower the risk of breakdown by spending $40 to $65 to have a qualified mechanic check out a car before you buy it.
- Check *Consumer Reports* as well as the blue book to learn the price you should be paying.
- Consider using the services of Car Bargains (800-475-7283; also available on America Online) for finding the best new car prices, though at $150 take this decision seriously. Consumer Automotive (703-631-5161) and Nationwide Auto Brokers (800-521-7257) also offer competitive prices for fees, very likely beating your dealer's best offer.

- Don't fill up with "premium" or "super" unleaded gas that costs an extra 20 cents a gallon unless your engine requires it. Most cars run on regular and cannot have their performance increased with higher octane fuel.

Should you lease a car? Leasing is *never* a better deal than buying a car and keeping it for many years. It is unfortunate that so many car buyers are more concerned with the monthly payment than the cost of the car. Leasing agencies take advantage of this fact by offering payments that may cost less than loan payments but leave you faced with the same decision of whether to buy or lease again, once you are paid up. Also, there can be several hidden charges in leasing contracts, such as the refundability of security deposits, lease termination fees of more than $500 for terminating early, mileage caps at 15,000 miles per year, and fees for "excess wear and tear," which can be a gray area. Some leasing companies are also charging substantial fees to cover property taxes on the value of their vehicles. And normally you will be stuck having to pay for *full* insurance coverage. Some people believe they will pay more over time in repairs when owning a car, but, with few exceptions, this is far from true. Buying a quality used car, maintaining it, driving it with care, and keeping it for more than ten years is by far the *most economical* choice.

STOP EATING MONEY, START EATING FOOD

The most essential item we must spend money on, even beyond housing, is food. Many spend more than triple what others do for the same result of satisfying, high-quality, and nutritious meals.

Aside from the direct cost of food is the cost of eating out. Being served outside the home can be a very pleasant and convenient experience. Eating out in a moderately decent restaurant, however, can cost as much as an entire week's groceries, just for *one meal*! If you now eat out twice a week, cut it in half, and learn about all the interesting and convenient ways to cook at home. Cooking good meals does not always have to be laborious and time-consuming. Quick, economical, and very nutritional recipes are available that will get your mouth watering with anticipation. Cutting down on eating out can save the average American family more than $1,000 a year. Spending $5 a day on lunch costs another $1,000 a year, which after ten years is $10,000, compared to the 75-cent daily cost of bagging your lunch.

Wisdom on Wealth

The most essential item we must spend money on, even beyond housing, is food. Many spend more than triple what others do for the same result of satisfying, high-quality, and nutritious meals.

I haven't forgotten the shock I experienced recently when I saw soft drinks for $2.50 in a movie theater, drinks that were 50 cents a can in the store across the street. I had known for years that I could buy nearly enough popcorn to fill a 55-gallon drum with what movie theaters charge for a couple of buckets. Have you ever contemplated how many $3.50 mixed drinks are made from one $10 bottle of liquor? I guarantee the bottle is still 80 percent full after it has been paid for! Similar high-profit margins can be found in foods purchased from vending machines, while much of this food is not of great quality. But nothing compares to bottled water, which costs from 200 to more than 1,000 times a drink from your tap, and often is no more pure.

The more packaging involved with food such as microwaveable dinners, the more it will cost. Maintaining food frozen is an expense consumers must pay for also. The cardboard, glass, plastic, and metal not only adds to the immediate cost for you and the food company but adds considerably to our trash dumps. Even if you are not a dedicated environmentalist, keep in mind that the removing and disposal of trash cost our country tens of billions of dollars a year. Lowering consumption, even in small ways, can help.

Many food companies provide buyer incentives through discount coupons, hoping to influence consumer habits, promote new products, or clear certain items that have not sold well. For items that you are going to purchase anyway, it would be downright foolish not to use coupons. And why not try something new once in a while? A poor choice is buying something you can wait for or don't really need, just because you have a coupon or the item was on sale. Occasionally, grocery stores double or triple the value of coupons. Also, sometimes store or generic brands are less than brand-name products even with a coupon. A family of four can average at least $20 a month in savings, minus the cost of the Sunday newspaper from which most of them come. Twenty dollars a month is $240 a year, and $2,400 in ten years which, if invested well, could accumulate to more than $6,000!

Here are a few more money-saving food tips:

- Come to the store with a list and a full stomach, and don't stray from your list unless you clearly forgot an essential item or happen to catch an excellent sale on a product you regularly buy. In grocery stores the items with the highest profit margins are placed in the most eye-catching places. An overpriced $4 box of cereal is going to be far more prominently displayed than a bag of rice.
- Some people think that buying packaged and frozen fruits and vegetables costs less, but this is rarely the case unless you can't eat fresh food fast enough before it spoils. Fresh usually costs less, especially when in season, and its nutritional content is higher. It tastes better and generates less trash.
- Thrift stores sell "day-old" bread and other baked goods that can be frozen. Stock up and make more efficient use of your freezer, which uses less power when full. Because bread now costs nearly $2 a loaf, a family of four can save at least another $20 a month.
- Rice and beans are very economical as well as being low in fat and sodium and very high in nutritional content.
- Don't buy health and beauty products in grocery stores—they are normally lower priced in discount department stores.
- Buying food in bulk not only saves money but time and transportation costs as well. Most individuals and families should be able to cut the number of trips to the grocery store to once a week, plus an extra trip for perishable foods. Going to several different stores to buy specific sale items, however, is not worth the extra time and gasoline, unless you are really stocking up. Some complain that purchasing a dozen jars of tomato sauce or juice, even at a 40 percent discount, will cut too deeply into their weekly or monthly food budget. If you average your food budget over several months, however, you will see that you can get a higher rate of return per month buying in bulk.
- Always use the *unit pricing* system, normally indicated by labeling along the bottom of the shelf under the product. This way, all you have to do is buy the product that has the lowest price per ounce or per pound. Because labeling is not always clear in some stores, carrying a pocket calculator can be handy. Divide the total price by the number of ounces or pounds to find the price per ounce or pound.

CUT COSTS ON CLOTHES AND FURNISHINGS

Although less essential than food, we all expect to have a reasonable amount of clothing and furnishings. Those who design and make their own clothes save a lot of money and can wear what they want, but this is not practical for most. Avoiding clothes that must be dry-cleaned can save you, on average, another $120 a year. There are many clothing consignment, thrift, and outlet stores that are worth investing some time and money in. Buying clothing off-season is a must for the thrifty shopper, if one can't find what he or she wants for even less at second-hand shops.

But the best bargains are at yard or garage sales and flea markets, not only for clothing, but for a variety of children's toys, household furnishings, tools, etc., which can be found in near-perfect condition. We have saved at least $1,000 on toddler clothing and toys and sometimes even find adult apparel for a dollar or two. Also check out the classified ads in newspapers. There are usually ads for people who must suddenly liquidate their material assets on divorce or death, where super-bargains can be found. I purchased a beautiful, like-new, solid oak entertainment center for $300, which would have cost me $799 plus tax in the store. That extra $500 was placed into a high-return investment years ago, now worth about $1,300, and by the time I am 65, could realistically be worth more than $45,000! Look for so-called defective or irregular items in stores, which can be marked down by up to 80 percent. Demonstration models that have had minimal use and come with full new product warranties can be excellent deals. I bought a demonstration Hewlett-Packard ink-jet printer marked down from $350 to just $230. Of course, there are good seasonal sales to make room for new inventory or boost sales during a slow period.

BUY QUALITY, NOT NAMES

With major appliances—TVs, stereos, VCRs, and computers—it's a good idea to buy them new, unless you are skilled at repairs. It is also worth buying high-quality, long-lasting models. The more features they have, however, the more things can break down. Many electronic appliances have more features than most of us use, so try to buy only what you need. Also, more complex machines are more costly to repair. Beware of buying some appliances largely because they have well-known names. Some names are well known more for their advertising and stylish appearance than their dependability. After only three years of very modest use, my Maytag washing machine needed a new motor switch at a cost of $127, including labor. The repairman informed me that exactly the same part for a Whirlpool or Kenmore machine would have only cost $18 instead of $80. Also, the initial cost of the Maytag was about $200 or 75 percent more than other brands. You may find the best price on some items through a mail-order catalog. Also, when it comes to technology, many pieces of equipment, such as computers for example, can become outdated quickly, so buy carefully. And never purchase products through rent-to-own arrangements via small weekly payments—the effective annual percentage rate can equal up to nearly $200 percent, costing you *more than triple* the actual price.

Frequently, salespeople will try to sell service contracts or extended warranties with the purchase of an appliance. These contracts are very profitable to appliance companies, which means *you* will profit greatly from not buying them. What few repairs may be needed normally cost less than the contract. And most of the time, quality merchandise will need *no repairs* during the warranty period. Look up repair records in *Consumer Reports*. Often by paying more, you only get a more expensive item that also costs more to repair.

Another option is to teach yourself repairs. However, with all the computer chips now found in electronic equipment, you may find that all you can learn is basic maintenance. There are still some ways consumers can cut corners. For example, you can buy cleaning supplies to clean your VCR for about $7, which will last for the life of the VCR. Electronics stores charge up to $80 for this ten-minute procedure.

PETS

According to the American Kennel Club, the total cost of owning a dog for 11 years averages $12,500, while having a cat for 15 years totals $5,600. Evaluate your pet needs and consider if such an expense can wait.

CUT YOUR OWN HAIR

Look into purchasing a hair-cutting kit, which costs $45 to $75, especially if you have a family. Learning to cut children's hair is easy and spouses can sometimes cut each other's hair as well. One friend of mine has learned to cut his own hair, even the back. Had he spent $10, plus transportation costs every two months at the barbershop for the past ten years, he would have spent $700. A typical family of four can average $400 a year on haircuts, not including perms or other specialized treatments. In ten years that is $4,000.

GIVE HOURS INSTEAD OF DOLLARS

Try giving your time and skills to charity instead of tithing in cash. Work can be appreciated just as much as money.

USING YOUR BANK WISELY

Having a bank account now often places one at a deficit, for guaranteed 5 percent interest is out, and highly personalized service is far from what many recall. According to a recent study by the Consumer Federation of America and the U.S. Public Interest Research Group, the cost to account holders of maintaining a typical bank account in 1993 averaged $184.16 annually. No doubt this is well over $200 now, because bank service charges have been increasing by average annual rates of nearly 15 percent for the last decade or so. In 1995, banks took in $16 billion in service charges. With this being the case, it is no wonder so many check-cashing places have sprung up. They fill the void for those who simply can't afford or realize that it is more to their advantage to not have a bank account. With ever more sophisticated computer systems, even tellers are gaining access to the profitability of customer accounts, permitting them to tailor the level of service charges on an individual basis.

Wisdom on Wealth

Banks nickel-and-dime you to death if you don't know how to play the game.

As I advise throughout this book, use fewer resources or use them more efficiently to achieve the same result. Here are the most profitable ways you can reduce or eliminate bank charges:

- Is your bank demanding that you maintain a balance of many hundreds or even thousands of dollars to be free of service charges? Keep in mind that a $1,000 balance in an account is a *nearly free loan* to your bank, which it can lend out at 6 percent to 12 percent while paying you 2 percent to 4 percent, a built-in service charge.
- Shop around. Generally, credit unions offer the best bargains, with small savings-and-loans in second place, and banks last. This rule applies to a full variety of banking services.
- Don't bounce checks. While the average cost to banks for returned checks is under $2, they gouge account holders for $15 to $35 each time. According to Consumer Loan Advocates in Lake Bluff, Illinois, banks now earn more than a billion dollars a year on this deal.
- Prevent charges for depositing worthless checks by cashing them at the bank the check is drawn from or at least call that bank to verify that there are sufficient funds to cover it.
- A few banks are charging fees to use a live teller. Circumvent this by using bank-by-telephone services, automatic deposit and draft and night deposit boxes, which are accessible 24 hours a day.
- Bank by mail with a bank such as USAA Federal Savings in San Antonio, Texas, 800-531-0520, which offers excellent banking services at about the most competitive rates in the industry.
- Avoid automated teller machines (ATMs) and their $1 to $2.50 per-transaction fees. Simply withdraw larger amounts less often and take advantage of the service offered by most grocery stores of being able to write checks for more than the amount of your purchases to get cash.
- Are you being charged a couple of dollars to transfer funds among accounts? Plan better and do it less often.
- It costs more to have the privilege of having checks returned with your statement at the end of the month. Consider how important this service is. How frequently have you had to prove a financial or legal matter in which a receipt would not perform the same function?
- Don't open an account if you intend to close it soon. If you need to close it, write a check to a friend or business for the remaining balance. Some banks charge up to $25 to close an account recently opened.

- Write fewer checks if charged per-check fees.
- Try to get overdraft protection in which overdrafts from checking accounts are automatically placed as a cash advance on a credit card or treated as a short-term loan, to avoid having to tie up cash in a savings account.
- How fast can you get access to your funds? Most checks fully clear the banking system within a few days, though your bank may have a holding period longer than this or hold a portion of the check for an extended time.
- Avoid stop-payment requests that can cost up to $15 by using credit cards for purchases that you believe may lead to problems getting credits or refunds.
- Be careful where you buy checks. Banks charge up to triple the cost of discount mail-order companies such as Current, 800-426-0822, and Image Checks, 800-562-8768, where I have ordered as many as 200 checks for under $5, including shipping.
- Don't ignore various types of debts such as some highway and parking fines, taxes, or other debtors you suspect might try to get access to your money. There have been cases of people having their bank accounts debited without prior notice, even though doing so is illegal.
- Don't transport large sums of cash. If stopped for a traffic violation or in an accident and the police happen to see $40,000 of cash in a popped-open briefcase, expect to be seriously questioned. Use cashier's checks or bank wire to prevent such hassles and have greater security.

ENJOY TRAVELING ECONOMICALLY

Once you have applied most of the money-saving advice presented in this book, you may find that in addition to having cash left over each month for long-term wealth building, you also can enjoy the luxury of a vacation. Many people think that a vacation means living it up, staying in fancy resort hotels, and spending a fortune on meals out, plane tickets, and rental cars. Some also believe they should not have to think about money while on a vacation, for this is the time to spend and enjoy.

Traveling cost-effectively depends largely on where and how far you are going, along with what promotions and incentives are available. Obviously, air travel saves the most time, but perhaps you prefer to

---

Wisdom on Wealth

A major goal of this book is to have economical thinking become so *automatic and positive* that it no longer will be dreaded or stressful, even when on vacation.

---

view the sights and scenes from the ground over a few days, rather than from 37,000 feet in the air for a couple of hours. Trips by train or bus can cost almost as much as by plane in some cases, but they allow those who prefer to stay on the ground an opportunity to reach their destination without having to drive. Crossing an ocean by ship can be an intriguing adventure and very relaxing if time is not a priority. Again, the costs vary and in some cases may be more than traveling by plane.

For those who have the time and like to drive, traveling by car is the least costly, especially with at least two people, and offers the most freedom. Gas, food, and lodging, however, can add up. To really slash the cost of driving, try advertising for riders to share expenses with at nearby colleges or universities or advertise yourself, if you want to join someone else. For some people, camping has proven an inexpensive alternative to motels. After the purchase of basic supplies for around $300, you will find camping offers a substantial savings. A motor home or towing trailer may well suit people who wish to spend a great deal of their time on the road or choose to make it their "permanent" residence.

One of the best ways to save money while traveling, however, is to take advantage of youth hostels. Now more than 5,500 youth hostels exist around the world, of which close to 300 are in the United States. They charge from as little as 50 cents a night in India to $18 a night per person in New York City. Couples, families, and singles of almost any age are welcome. Hostels do not offer the same level of privacy as hotels and motels do, but they are clean, comfortable, and a great way to meet other interesting travelers. Rooms are dormitory style with several beds to a room, and bathrooms and telephones are down the hall. You can save even more money by cooking your own food in the kitchen. As of 1997, membership in American Youth Hostels is only $15 to $40 a year, depending on your category. Some hostel managers will let travelers work off their board by cleaning, painting, mowing the lawn, or performing other handiwork on occasion. American Youth

Hostels headquarters may be contacted at 202-783-2294. Some colleges and universities rent out their dormitory rooms during the summer when vacant at very low prices as well.

Another great way to save a fortune on lodging if you're staying in one area for an extended time is to arrange a house swap. The two most well-known exchange guides in which you can list your home and search for others are published by Vacation Exchange Club, 800-638-3841, and Intervac, 800-756-4663. They charge about $70 for a listing in one of three guides published yearly. You must contact potential swaps yourself and the companies listed won't be held responsible for any problems you might have, although they will delete any problem candidates that you report. Generally, people try to find others who lead similar lifestyles, evaluating them on cleanliness, smoking preference, pets, etc., in addition to availability and location. Normally, your homeowner's insurance covers nonpaying guests, but call your agent just to be sure. A lot of mutual trust is involved in these arrangements, but a simple contract that covers basic areas such as security, car use, maintenance and upkeep, and how to handle emergencies, is essential. More than 9,000 houses are listed, primarily in the United States, Canada, Mexico, and Western Europe.

NEVER FLY FULL PRICE

For great deals on plane fares here are a few basic rules you should know. Airfares change daily as airlines compete to keep their planes full to maximize their efficiency. Ultimately, your level of determination and flexibility, what you are willing to pay, and how good a shopper you are can have more bearing on the ticket price than the cost to the airline of filling the seat. The variety of prices for the same flight is mind-boggling.

There are several strategies for finding the lowest fares. First try calling three major airlines with your flight plans and write down their ticket prices without booking anything. Then try an experienced travel agent. You want an agent who is willing to spend the time to play with various arrangements. Keep in mind, however, that travel agents earn their money on commissions so if some rate quotes seem questionable, you may want to call the airlines yourself. Airline reservationists are not trained to offer creative options, nor have the time. Travel agents are and will make the time if they want your business. If you can get a "yes" for at least seven of the following questions, you've found a good travel agent.

- Are they comfortable booking hidden-city flights (stopping at another destination besides the one signed up for)?
- Do they subscribe to the OAG (Official Airline Guide) electronic tariff system?
- Are they certified as travel agents?
- Are they members of the American Society of Travel Agents (ASTA)?
- Will they rebate commissions? Most don't, but it never hurts to ask. Try calling Travel Avenue, 312-876-1116, or 800-FLY CHEAP, which may charge a nominal fee for ticket processing while rebating amounts much greater or offering steep discounts.
- Do they have access to consolidators, wholesalers, and bucket shops?
- Do they have an independent auditing program to continually search for lower fares?
- Do they use five computer reservation systems (CRSs) and Southwest's internal system?
- Do they have a 24-hour toll-free telephone number?

As annoying as some of the airline restrictions are to get the lower fares, it is well worth accommodating yourself to them. Here are some cost-cutting airline tips to consider:

- The time of year: Airfares change with holidays and the seasons; factors in the economy and competition can contribute to potentially drastic changes in fare structures. A whole variety of discount coupons are available from numerous sources. One family I know got $150 worth of discount coupons from three boxes of cereal. Nearly all travel clubs offer discounts on hotels, airfares, train tickets, and rental cars of between 5 percent and 15 percent. For those who travel at least every year, a subscription to *Best Fares* magazine is well worth the $58 annual price, 800-880-1234, or *Inside Flyer*, 800-333-5937. These magazines are packed with information on bargain rates throughout the travel industry, from airline discounts to car rental, cruises, hotels, and tons more. Senior-citizen discounts are widely available also. Paying full listed or "rack" rates for all major travel services is never necessary. Simply calling The Room Exchange at 800-846-7000 can chop off 20 percent to 50 percent of hotel rates at more than 22,000 locations in most of North America.

- Purchasing your ticket when you book your flight can lock in a low fare so if you get a great deal, fork over the funds. It's better to use a charge card because, by law, airlines must refund purchases within seven days on customer request (which is handled more efficiently with a credit card), some cards offer free flight/life insurance, and others provide up to 5 percent off ticket prices or air miles. If you are flying a lot over a certain period of time, look into purchasing unlimited flight travel for 30-, 60-, or 90-day time slots, which is far less costly than paying separately. And keep in mind that *where* you book tickets internationally can have a considerable effect on ticket prices, even for identical flights.
- Fares to major cities are generally less costly than fares to a smaller city nearby. Airlines know they can fill planes traveling to large, well-known cities. If a plane stops in the place you want to travel to, you may find it cheaper to buy tickets for a flight that eventually lands at another destination. This concept is called hidden-city booking. For example, if the fare from Chicago to San Francisco is $400 with a stopover in Salt Lake City but the fare from Chicago to Salt Lake City is $450, you might as well buy the ticket to San Francisco and get off in Salt Lake City. For one-way flights this strategy works fine; for round-trip flights, it can get considerably more complicated. Once a seat shows as empty, in this case the return flight from San Francisco to Salt Lake City, the airline has the right to fill that seat. You could try buying two one-way tickets, but one-way domestic fares are usually no less than round-trip tickets. You can always fly into a neighboring city round trip, skipping the last leg of the flight to the larger city, which most likely the flight is to (carry on all your bags) and rent a car, if the price of gas and the car rental is cheaper than the remaining flight or have a friend meet you. An example of this strategy is getting off in Colorado Springs with a Denver destination.
- Airlines frequently overbook flights assuming that they will have a certain percentage of cancellations or no-shows. Most of the time their assumptions are correct, but when you are bumped to another flight, it can be to your advantage. Most of the major airlines will give out very generous offers, even free round-trip tickets to anywhere in the country, if a passenger is bumped. They are legally required to give you half the cost of your ticket, up to $200, if you arrive more than an hour late to your destination or double if you're more than two hours late. For international flights, it's a four-hour delay in arrival, although this does not ap-

ply for incoming international flights. Bumping is most likely to occur during busy holiday times, although I normally don't recommend flying at those times because specially discounted fares are rarely available.

For travel to funerals of *immediate* relatives, you can take advantage of bereavement fares that are much lower than standard prices, though you may have to be reimbursed for the difference after paying full fare.

Suppose your plane is diverted to another airport far from your intended destination? Or what do you do if you miss a connecting flight? If such inconveniences are clearly the fault of the airline, the airline normally will put you up for free in a hotel and pay for your meals until the next available flight can be arranged. If major delays are caused by weather problems, such generosity rarely applies. Should you miss a flight because of your own irresponsibility, airlines have the right to void your ticket completely, although usually they can work out a reasonable arrangement for a slight charge.

SAVING ON RENTAL CARS

In many cases, after flying you will expect to rent a car. Rental-car rates vary considerably, depending on many factors, including the agency, season, and the part of the country the car is being rented in. Be sure to inquire about the destination fee if you are considering leaving the car elsewhere than where you rented it. I have never forgotten the time I returned a car a day early on a week rental with a well-known rental chain that tried to charge me an *early return fee*. Fortunately, I had booked the car through the use of a voucher with a travel club, not a credit card, so I stuck to my own set of ethics. I ignored the threats of damaged credit, which never occurred, and walked out.

Be sure to ask what the policy is on leaving the gas tank empty— rental agencies will charge you up to 100 percent more than the standard per-gallon price for the gas if they have to fill the tank. If the insurance you have on your personal automobile covers you in a rental (as most policies do) don't buy redundant insurance. If you don't have collision or theft insurance, you should get some because rentals are usually almost new and would be extremely costly to replace or repair. Unfortunately, rental-car insurance rates are quite high. Usually your credit card offers this coverage for free and could save you about $10 a day. For long-distance trips, be sure to get unlimited mileage in your contract. Mileage fees can add up fast. And beware of the higher cost of renting cars overseas. Rates abroad can be double to triple the domestic rates in many cases. Use public transportation more.

OTHER TRAVEL ALTERNATIVES

In addition to carpooling to save money on travel, you can drive a car across the country and not pay a dime! There are companies in the business of moving motor vehicles from one part of the country to another. They are often looking for drivers, and in some cases, cover your gas expenses. Sometimes these services ask you to deliver recreational vehicles, in which case you can sleep in the vehicle and save motel costs. These companies can be found under the heading of "transportation" in newspaper classifieds and in the yellow pages.

Lots of tour organizations offer good rates because they book many people at once. The best deal is to sponsor a minimum number of other people, usually at least five to eight, because they can travel for free or very close to it. Such tours are common for high school and college students. Postings can be found in school offices and college student centers, and of course in your library. Some tours focus on a particular topic and others are more oriented toward sheer pleasure, entertainment, and tourism. Unless you have a high degree of familiarity with a foreign country, I highly recommend going with a tour group because it can offer you greater security, friendship, and financial savings.

Wisdom on Wealth

Again, as with housing, you can travel from virtually free to very expensively to visit the same places, depending to what extent you are willing to seek out alternatives, do research, be creative, and sometimes put up with what may be minor inconveniences.

Beware of losing money on exchanging currencies. Credit cards are essential for foreign travel. And with so many ATM machines popping up around the world, their convenience is now starting to surpass traveler's checks. To access a menu of Cirrus machines call 800-424-7787. For VISA or Plus System ATM locations, check out this Internet web site: http://www.visa.com. With MasterCard or VISA, you can call your issuing bank for information as well.

So can you afford the luxury of seeing the country and much of the world? Most definitely! Analyze your real motive to travel. If you are visiting a foreign country primarily to see the sights and get a feel for the culture, modest accommodations may be adequate and allow you to do a lot more on a limited budget.

Once you have adjusted your budget so you can stay out of debt and pay yourself a sum each month, take some of this savings and occasionally go on a wonderful vacation. By living a quality lifestyle on less, you can have access to much of what is traditionally assumed to be only luxuries for the more wealthy. The $125 suit you purchase in a consignment store that has the same quality as the $1,300 suit at the men's shop pays you back twofold: It serves the same function as the $1,300 suit and permits you to be on the same plane with your favorite movie star, basketball player, or news anchor. As demonstrated throughout the chapter, this principle applies to spending in nearly all areas.

Wisdom on Wealth

Remember that wealth is not merely determined by your net worth and income but by your *quality of life*.

CHAPTER 10

Money-Saving Tips for College and Weddings

If you are preparing to pay for your college education or that of your children, it is essential to realize that this expense may be the most costly item you may ever pay for other than your home. As with everything else, however, there are expensive ways and economical ways to get a quality college education. The media commonly refers to figures of up to half a million dollars to put two children through college in another 10 to 15 years. If these figures were true, many would feel justifiably frustrated. You don't, however, have to resign yourself to not being able to afford college. According to the College Board's 1995 figures, 30 percent of students paid less than $2,000 a year for tuition and fees and 75 percent paid under $4,000 at four-year public colleges and universities, while 66 percent of students enrolled at private colleges paid less than $12,000 a year.

According to the College Board's annual report, *Trends in Student Aid 1985–1995*, $46.8 billion in financial aid was available to college students in the 1994–1995 school year, some as loans and some as grants. Unfortunately for some, the trend is for less money to come in the form of grants—and then only for the most needy—and more money to come in as loans with less subsidies. Though the rate of increase in college costs has leveled off in recent years, it is still close to 6 percent per year, according to College Board statistics. Colleges must compete to get good students and keep top-notch professors and, therefore, must keep increasing salaries and purchasing state-of-the-art equipment.

Wisdom on Wealth

Knowing how to navigate the financial-aid maze, implementing your own economical lifestyle methods, and wisely investing can help you to tackle the college cost challenge.

CREATIVE LIFESTYLE STRATEGIES

By the time children are in their teens, parents can normally tell if they are college-bound or not. Not all people are meant to attend college or some may only plan to attend for two years, instead of four. Some may perform better in a trade, may be too creative for traditional school, or may have the opportunity to go into business for themselves. If you have invested for many years and now your child is not going to college, these earmarked funds can be wisely diverted to other needs. If you do have children planning on going to college, here are a few ways you can cut college costs:

- If you have children who are exceptionally academic, perhaps they can take College Board *College Level Examination Program* (CLEP) tests to exempt them from college courses or take college credit courses during summers in high school. Doing so can potentially save you a couple of thousand dollars.
- Look into correspondence schools or local community college classes offered on cable TV. Community colleges are great resources and good money savers for required courses, often with smaller, more personalized class settings than universities. However, you may not be able to transfer full credit hours for some community college courses or courses taught in alternative circumstances or they may only show as pass/fail. Check out your school's policies before enrolling. Some colleges offer credit for exceptional life experiences, too.
- Can your children live *at home* rather than have separate housing? Many schools have commuter opportunities that can save you a lot of money.

- Many colleges will permit students to complete degrees in three instead of four years, which can save a fortune if the student can handle full loads of courses 12 months a year for three years.
- A few colleges and universities offer "cooperative education" in which the school finds work related to the student's field of study and rotates it with a student's course work. Cooperative education can cover a large portion of costs and provide excellent work experience (Northeastern University in Boston, for example, offers this option).
- If children insist on moving out, can they work during summers or part-time or implement some of the economical housing methods mentioned in Chapter 6? My wife house-sat, assisted the elderly, and cleaned house for three out of four years of college, saving herself thousands of dollars. Student housing offices and college newspapers often list such opportunities.

More parents are being enticed by college prepayment plans that guarantee full payment of certain amounts up to a complete four-year degree. The sense of security this concept offers is comforting and provides a level of discipline to savers. With some rather basic knowledge of investing, however, you can do better with your own tailored investment plan. Some banks offer "college CDs" also, which are along the same idea as the other prepayment plans. Though prepayment plans generally must return most or all of your money if your child ends up not attending college, some don't pay the interest accumulated that could be extremely costly compared to your own investment plan.

Also, consider buying Series EE U.S. savings bonds which, if purchased after December 31, 1989, qualify for tax-exemption of their interest up to certain income limits when applied toward tuition and fees for students under the age of 24 who are U.S. citizens. These plans still can't compare to the returns of aggressive stock funds, regardless of taxes. The prepaid plans are not exclusive of tax considerations, either.

GRANTS, LOANS, AND SCHOLARSHIPS

Information on grants, loans, and scholarships is covered in depth by volumes of material available in high school guidance offices, college libraries, and bookstores. Here are some tips to remember while researching your options:

- Now, more than ever, it is a priority to fill out and mail in financial-aid applications *early*. As of the 1996–97 school year, at least 450 colleges and universities are accepting applications as early as October, *three months sooner* than in the past. Much of the best aid is handed out on a first come–first served basis, so don't cost yourself a fortune by procrastinating. Call the College Scholarship Service at 609-771-7725 for information.

- This application consists of the required Free Application for Federal Student Aid (FAFSA), which is computerized to estimate eligibility for federal grants and loans, state grants and loans, and work-study jobs.

- A video on the financial-aid application process that parents and students can view is available at most high school guidance offices.

- Colleges base the amount of aid offered on their costs and what they expect you can contribute. A formula calculates the age of parents, household income, assets, family size, number of children in college, if the student is considered independent (24 years of age by December 31 of the year in which aid is awarded), marital and veteran status of the student, and some extenuating circumstances such as divorce or a medical problem. Disability and/or unemployment and your debt load will be taken into account also.

- Should a college assume that *both* parents will contribute, and this is not the case, request a Divorced/Separated Parents Statement from the College Board, 212-713-8000, which you must send directly to the college. If child-support payments have not been provided, indicate this as well.

- Beware that financial-aid eligibility is determined at a *much higher* rate for assets in the student's name than in the parents' name (35 percent instead of 5.7 percent). So for those parents who have been taking advantage of the preferred tax status of children's custodial accounts, you should funnel most of those funds back into *your* account before applying for college aid. This strategy could get a little sticky with the Internal Revenue Service, but it can be accomplished legally, especially with the child's consent.

- Some private schools may require filing a CSS/Financial Aid Profile administered by the College Board for a modest fee, which contains questions tailored to the individual school and may require parents to reveal more details about their assets than the FAFSA.

- The most elite private schools may have their own financial-aid eligibility forms.
- Don't reveal any income or assets not asked for. Depending on the form, retirement accounts, life insurance policies, annuities, and trust accounts may be exempt. Defer year-end bonuses and royalties to reduce your reportable income for the year in which aid is being applied for.
- Bargain hard. Colleges are competing for the best students. Many people are bidding between schools now, which is a great strategy to try. I have seen initial aid offers multiplied tenfold or more.
- Try to get as much in *grants and work study* as possible rather than loans that must be paid back. The standard grants are the Pell, awarded by the government, and the Supplemental Educational Opportunity Grant (SEOG), awarded to undergraduates by the school.
- Explore military options. Check out the Reserve Officers' Training Corps (ROTC) program in high school. This involves continued summer training and a minimum service commitment after college. A modest amount of time in the military can provide generous grants via the GI Bill that can cover entire degrees also, as well as military academies. Grade point averages of at least 3.6 are usually required.
- Inquire what can be expected through the four years—aid has a way of diminishing after the first year.
- Apply for scholarships, though keep in mind that their value most likely will be subtracted from other aid awards, which is one reason why billions of dollars of grant money go unclaimed each year.
- Do not use financial aid/scholarship search firms to locate funds. They charge a couple of hundred dollars (normally refundable if an equal amount of aid is not found) to accomplish what you can easily do yourself.
- Use the computer database, Fund Finder, compiled by the College Board, and available in many high school guidance offices and on the College Board's World Wide Web site.
- Negotiate a price guarantee with the college of choice that will keep costs within reasonable inflation limitations.
- Once parent and child contributions, grants, and work-study aid is added up, the remainder must come in the form of *loans*.

- The Stafford loan is a loan taken out by students in their name with caps of about $2,650 for their first year to nearly $9,000 per year in graduate school. If students are able to claim themselves as independent, they can double the borrowing limits. An advantage to Staffords is that payments don't start until six months after graduation while the government pays interest in the meantime.
- The PLUS (Parent Loan for Undergraduate Students) is a college loan taken out by parents in which the only borrowing limit is the parents' creditworthiness.
- The Perkins loan is a low-interest federal loan for undergraduates and graduate students with financial need. This is awarded by the school and does not have to start being paid back until nine months after graduation and is canceled in cases of death, permanent disability, or commitments to volunteer to qualifying organizations.
- Shop around for loans—banks vary the frequency of interest compounding and offer various incentives for timely paying and loan-repayment methods.
- Keep in mind that part of certain loans (several hundred dollars) goes to insure them, leaving less to make use of, which indirectly raises the actual interest rate you pay.
- Look into getting a home equity loan (not available in Texas), the interest on which is tax deductible.
- To locate college-aid lenders in your area, call a local college financial-aid office. For the New England Educational Loan Marketing Corporation (Nellie Mae) call 800-634-9308, for the Student Loan Marketing Association (Sallie Mae) call 800-874-9390, and try the Academic Management Services at 800-635-0120.
- You can defer your loan payments for up to three years after graduation, though interest will continue to accumulate.
- Lenders are required to allow up to 24 months of "hardship forbearance." Again, however, interest is not forgiven.
- Defaulting on student loans is *not wise*. If your loans are from the government, the IRS can withhold tax refunds to help pay them and wages can be garnished. Defaulting can also affect your credit rating.

WEDDING: ROMANCE AND DEBT DON'T MIX

At some point in your life, you or your children may meet someone very special and decide to get married. You may wish to have a ceremonious wedding. Walking in and out of the courthouse in a few minutes and dropping a small check may not be exactly what you have in mind, though it is as legal as a $40,000 wedding, and a lot more practical.

The majority of families still expect to have a traditional wedding with most of the formalities. Their attitude is "You only do it once, nothing is as special as love, and for once, cost just shouldn't be a significant concern." Wedding costs, however, can quickly add up. In fact, the bridal market alone contributes significantly to the U.S. economy, with an estimated total of just over $34 *billion* a year. Nearly $3 billion a year is spent on rings alone! In 1997, the average price of a wedding will be $17,000, approximately the price of a new car.

Wisdom on Wealth

With money as the primary source of turmoil in adult relationships, starting marriage with burdensome bills to pay is a wedding anticlimax no one needs. I simply believe in starting marriage as *debt-free* as possible and paying for wedding expenses in *cash*, whether it's your first marriage or not.

Can you have a beautiful, romantic wedding without the financial letdown looming overhead? Definitely! First of all, regardless of tradition, I believe that *both* families should contribute somewhat equally. This seems only fair, especially if both are in financial positions to do so. Unfortunately, there are circumstances when one set of parents may not respect their son's or daughter's choice and becomes less generous or not very negotiable.

ELEGANT BUT NOT OUTRAGEOUS

Here is a list of how you can have a quality wedding without sinking into debt afterward:

- Set an upper spending limit and stick to it. Splurge on what is the most important. Economize on the rest.
- Choose to marry off-season. A Sunday afternoon in October is going to cost less than a Saturday evening in June for most services.
- A high-quality diamond ring can be purchased at the most expensive store in New York for $4,800 or for $500 at a pawn shop in New Mexico (a diamond loses half its value when a jewelry store cashier hands you your receipt). *Your* bottom line? Is the ring and stone *beautiful* to both of you, is the diamond *real*, and is it properly set, and is the ring at least 14-carat gold? (Fourteen carat is harder and holds up better than higher grades.)
- Consider getting an appraisal of the diamond from a gemologist certified by the American Society of Appraisers, American Gemological Society, or other qualified organizations.
- Place a limit on your guest list by inviting only those most special to you.
- Consider holding the ceremony and the reception in a friend's beautiful, private yard for rock-bottom economy.
- If this can't be arranged, try renting a portion of a municipal park that generally costs $50 to $250. Historic homes are another moderately priced alternative.
- Stay out of pricey city hotels and large, established churches, though small-town churches may be very reasonable.
- By serving lunch instead of dinner, up to 20 percent can be shaved off your food budget. Buffets may cost less, especially if you limit the exotic stuff and choose locally grown, in-season fruits and vegetables.
- To go real economy class on food, have a couple of your most trusted friends/relatives assist a day or two ahead in buying, preparing, and storing food. (At least use this strategy for the *rehearsal* dinner.) Then hire people to set it up and serve it.
- As opposed to an open bar that can cost up to $10 per person, buy your own beer, wine, soft drinks, and spring water by the case ahead of time and have your food servers pour drinks as well.

- As for the cake, have your baker fake the first layer or two with frosted Styrofoam, which can save $100 to $300, depending on the size of the cake.
- Try buying a dress the following ways: the clothing consignment store, classified ads in newspapers, rent or borrow one, have a friend who is handy with a sewing machine make one, wear a nice but nontraditional dress that can also be worn at future occasions, order a dress from Discount Bridal Service, 800-874-8794, which sells direct for up to 40 percent off, or take advantage of a closeout or special sale at stores such as Filene's Basement.
- For bride's and groom's mothers' and bridesmaids' dresses, apply the most appropriate of these strategies.
- Other than the groom, consider having the ushers and best man dress down.
- Look into hiring a disc jockey to keep music flowing at half the cost of a live band. Be sure the person you hire has wedding experience. For greater savings, set up quality CD players and extension speakers that you may own or can borrow.
- Hire the photographer to shoot only the ceremony and some good still shots but skip the reception when some of your friends and relatives can take over with their own cameras and perhaps a camcorder. To further economize, take the risk of having lower quality photos by *only* having attendees shoot.
- For photo processing, look up mail-order photo labs in photography magazines where I have found prices as low as under $5 for 11 × 14s, under $2 for 8 × 10s, and under $1 for 5 × 7s. You may have to wait about a month to see your pictures, however. With local labs charging five to ten times these prices, money is more valuable than time.
- Call around to flower *wholesalers* where, by placing a bulk order, you may save up to 50 percent off the cost of flowers at a retail florist shop. Limit the types of flowers. Fifteen brilliant tulips for $20 will be appreciated more than one $20 Hawaiian orchid. To more deeply economize, if in season, pick some of your own wild flowers or garden flowers.
- Regarding wedding invitations, you can pay up to $8 each for engraved invitations with reply cards and envelopes, or as little as about $1 each for thermographically printed cards by ordering them by mail from American Stationery Co. in Peru, Indiana, 800-428-0379, or Rexcraft in Rexburg, Idaho, 800-635-3898. These

prices are based on a minimum order of 100. Call around to check out competition. Also try seeing what your color ink-jet or laser printer can do, if you are so equipped or know someone who is.

- Consider whether you need to use a limousine service if another clean, late-model vehicle is available with a dependable driver.
- Buy the attendant gifts at the same store. With this large a purchase, if you can't bargain for a discount, go elsewhere.
- The bulk-buying principle should also apply if booking several hotel rooms.
- Stay within budget for the honeymoon. Whether it's the spectacular national parks out west, Hawaii, New England, or a cruise to the Bahamas, a couple should be able to take a lovely honeymoon for under $1,000.

TO HAVE OR NOT HAVE A PRENUP

A prenuptial marriage contract is similar to a will in the sense that it is designed for the purpose of preserving and directing assets in the event of a divorce. With the divorce rate as high as it is, prenuptial contracts have become more popular. For young couples marrying for their first time who have few assets and no children, these contracts are less appropriate and may offend either partner.

With older partners who are planning their marriage, a prenuptial may be appropriate because older people are more likely to have accumulated substantial assets, children from a previous marriage, aging parents to care for, a possible looming fortune from an inheritance, own a business, and other responsibilities. With the divorce rate in second marriages even higher than in first ones, the need is even greater. With a properly drawn contract, legal representation from both sides, and complete, honest financial disclosure from both parties, a prenuptial agreement can be very enduring.

In brief, here are the major reasons for a prenuptial contract:

- Being protected from a spouse's creditors
- Making divorce proceedings flow more easily
- Keeping assets that were yours before marrying
- Protecting rights to future spousal earnings
- Protection of your future earning potential
- Protecting financial needs of children from a prior relationship
- Checking out changes that may have to be made in wills

- Inheritance protection
- Possible compensation for having to give up a job
- Protection of business assets and legal snooping

So, if you are a young adult and are considering attending college or getting married, hold some practical kitchen table meetings in which economical and productive negotiations are made. Lay out realistic plans with possible alternates, stopgap measures, and safety nets to cover potential pitfalls. Major financial blunders are serious at any age. Money wasted while young is lost opportunity (value of funds that could be worth a fortune in the future), while money misspent at an older age is money with less time to recoup. If you are a parent or close friend, try to be involved in assisting in these major decisions, hopefully adding a touch of wisdom, objectivity, and common sense to such matters in which emotions can override practicality, especially among young people.

Wisdom on Wealth

Major financial blunders are serious at any age. Money wasted while young is lost opportunity (value of funds that could be worth a fortune in the future), while money misspent at an older age is money with less time to recoup.

CHAPTER 11

Investing Strategies to Grow Your Savings

After eliminating all your high-interest debt and becoming wiser on how to save money, you may start to have some cash left over each month. Understanding *where* to place this extra cash is critical and is the *other half* of wealth building. Investing involves placing your money into the hands of others with the expectation that, at some future time, the money you've invested will be worth considerably more than it is now. Yet, clearly you don't want to risk having the value of your money *decrease*. Too much of your life went into earning it to throw it away!

Wisdom on Wealth

Investing involves placing your money into the hands of others with the expectation that, at some future time, the money you've invested will be worth considerably more than it is now.

GETTING RESULTS AND TOLERATING RISK

The goal of investors is to obtain the maximum return on their money in the least amount of time with the least amount of risk. Unfortunately, maximum returns, short amounts of time, and low risk *don't* work together most of the time. With the exception of some anomalies, the more risk in an investment, the greater the potential for higher or lower returns. For many, the word *risk* immediately conjures up images of losing large sums of money, as happened in the stock market crash of 1929. The 1990s have little resemblance to 1929. For those who are willing to use time and knowledge to their advantage, moderate levels of risk are well worth taking, especially in the short-term. I emphasize short-term, for fluctuations are far more likely to occur in a few weeks or months in many growth investments than over many years. Time and money are *very* interrelated and must work together to be most effective. You don't want to be too old to enjoy money, nor do you want to end up with too little of it.

YOUR BANK WILL NOT MAKE YOU WEALTHY

When deciding where to invest your money, consider the following factors:

- The amount of money you want to accumulate for what purpose
- The length of time your goals are set for
- The reputation of the institution and/or broker who places your funds
- Your income tax bracket and various tax strategy considerations
- Expectations of future earnings
- Your tolerance for short-term substantial value fluctuations
- Your level of desire to reach financial independence
- Whether you want a steady flow of monthly income or asset capital appreciation

The most familiar places millions of people leave their savings in are banks, savings and loans, and credit unions, which as of the mid-1990s, are paying a 3 percent to 4 percent annual return. Because these returns approximate the inflation rate in the United States, money left in these accounts is not earning you much of anything. The only benefits of these accounts are the federal insurance protection of up to $100,000 per account and the instant access you have to your money. Your return can be increased a couple of percentage points by buying certif-icates of deposit that lock up your money for an agreed-on time. Mini-mums usually start at $500 for six months. Larger amounts of money for longer periods may buy you another point. Money market accounts normally provide slightly less of a return than CDs but a little higher return than regular savings rates. Banks turn right around and loan your cash out at 8 percent to 14 percent. You can, too. Enter the world of *investing!*

Wisdom on Wealth

Relying on a few basic rules will assist you in feeling confident that your investments represent security rather than fear. First of all, you must set short-term goals of under three years, moderate-term goals of three to ten years, and long-term goals of more than ten years.

THE RULES

Generally, longer-term investing will achieve greater returns on an annual basis than shorter-term investing because of compound inter-est. Of course, there are some exceptions when certain investments need to be sold early on. Also, many investments cost you *buy-and-sell commissions*, which reduce potential gains, especially if buying and selling frequently.

Here are a few general words of caution regarding investments. It is rarely worth listening to exciting rumors of investment opportunities, because by the time you can act on them they may have already gone from green to ripe and perhaps to rotten. Most of all, it is essential not to be excessively controlled by greed. Years ago, I invested in a gold mine stock that my broker was raving about. I bought it at $5 a share. Within a month it reached $50. Making such high returns in only a month should have satisfied my broker and myself! The broker said he thought my stock would rise to more than $100 a share the next month. Six weeks later it was at $3 a share and stayed in the $2 to $3 range for years. This is an extreme example of how you can gain and lose money quickly by investing in the stock market.

Another rule is to keep aware of economic changes in both the nation and around the world as they relate to your investments. Economic forecasts and statistics are in the news frequently, far more than most people can keep up with. Some investments demonstrate spectacular performances in a recessionary climate while others thrive under high inflation, high or low interest rates, new tax law changes, or even during a war. Major moves in one's investment strategies can be based on trends but should not be implemented hastily, for new economic reports are issued almost daily.

Wisdom on Wealth

Highly rewarding investing comes to those who are *patient and understand* the virtues of long-term investing. This fact naturally provides younger people with more potential for increasing their wealth.

How much money do you want to have by when and for what purposes? How much will it take to generate what amount of dependable income each month? Most of us want all the money we can get but it is only appropriate to be realistic. Stay within the boundaries of your income, how much you can expect it to rise, what your level of expenses are now and what they will be in the future, and your age. With the information presented here, you can set up a quality investment plan on your own without paying for the advice of a professional beyond the cost of this book.

THE LAWS OF MATHEMATICS CAN MAKE YOU WEALTHIER THAN YOUR PAYCHECKS

By starting to save an affordable portion of your paycheck *now* and investing it properly for many years, it is possible to create more investment income than your salary provides or certainly a great supplement to your retirement pension and/or Social Security. It is conceivable that someone earning only the *minimum wage* throughout his or her entire working life and investing 10 percent of it could be a millionaire by the age of 65 or earlier. Most likely, people will increase their earnings and move up the pay scale, which adds even greater savings potential. For example, just the cost of a pack of cigarettes each day, if invested at 12 percent annually for 30 years, accumulates to more than $185,000!

If you have trouble keeping within your budget, you might make a game out of avoiding purchasing something unnecessary and instead pay off a small bill to a department store. If the bill is not small, chip away at it over a period of time. Once you have tackled high-interest debt such as credit cards, take the money you were placing toward the debt and start a monthly investment plan. If you are confident that you can sustain a monthly savings of at least a minimum amount, contact a reputable no-load stock mutual fund and arrange an automatic investment plan, which many funds will do for as little as a $50 investment a month. Consider if your tax bracket and other aspects of your financial profile are appropriate for your investment to be in an IRA or other tax-deferred retirement plan or split your savings deduction between a couple of funds, one as an IRA and another as a regular account. Soon you will see how much pleasure you can get out of watching your money grow into your dreams. Start now!

EXAMPLES OF THE POWER OF COMPOUNDING

One convenient tool of basic math called the "rule of 72s" is very handy for knowing how quickly your money will double. Simply divide 72 by the percent of the interest rate you are receiving on your money. For example, it will take 72 years for your money to double at the rate of 1 percent per year. A 6 percent return will double your money in 12 years because 72 divided by 6 equals 12. At 15 percent annually it will take 4 years and 10 months, and at 20 percent, 3 years and 7 months.

Time and money work together as follows:

Let's say that you would like to have $100,000 at the age of 65. If you start at the age of 25 and average 12% annual return, you will have to pack away only $10.22 out of your paycheck each month, assuming tax deferral. But if you wait until the age of 45 to start, you will have to save just over $100 a month and by the age of 55 you would have to put away almost $450 a month to reach exactly the same goal. What is more rewarding than having your money and time work for you independently? The age-old expression, "One must have money to make money," is still true, but what is important here is that one doesn't have to *earn* much money to have money. Here are some other examples of what I call the time/money continuum.

Saving just $1 a day, starting at the age of 25, and having it compound at 12% annually will equal $296,000+ by the age of 65, but if you wait only *one more year* to start, your total will be $32,000 less, and if you wait until the age of 30 to start, it will cost you almost $180,000!

Wisdom on Wealth

Clearly, procrastination can be *very* expensive.

Another potentially expensive decision, if not properly selected for the goal intended, is *where* to place your savings because the rate at which it compounds can have as large an effect on the final result as the amount of time over which it accumulates.

For example: Investing $100 a month at 5 percent annual return will provide very different results than if compounded at 10 percent, 12 percent, 15 percent, or 20 percent.

	5 Years	15 Years	20 Years	30 Years	35 Years
5%	$6,801	$26,729	$ 41,103	$ 83,226	$ 113,609
10%	7,744	41,447	75,937	222,049	379,664
12%	8,176	49,958	98,926	349,496	643,096
15%	8,857	66,851	149,724	692,328	1,467,718
20%	9,867	95,432	247,241	1,554,301	3,867,600

Now let's look at what a one-time lump sum could result in without adding another dime to it. For simplicity, I am using the round figure of $1,000.

	10 Years	30 Years	50 Years
5%	$1,628	$ 4,322	$ 11,467
12%	3,106	29,960	289,002

Yes, virtually anyone can accumulate wealth, lots of it. If your goal is to use less time, energy, and money to accomplish the same or greater level of satisfaction in life, then understanding and implementing a savings investment plan that maximizes the power of compounding will ensure you achieve that goal.

Although understanding the value of compounding over time is extremely valuable, without sustained self-discipline to lay the foundation, this knowledge will be of little benefit. There are those with PhDs in mathematics and others with MBAs with high incomes who view this information as elementary. Yet how many have the discipline to reach highly prosperous goals? The bottom line is the value of your liquid assets in measuring your immediate financial capacity or level of general purchasing power. You *must* take responsibility for your financial well-being. By doing so, you will realize at some point that you can spend more of your life engaging in that which rewards you personally by choice.

INVESTMENT REVIEW

Here are the common categories of investments, their intended purposes, and their potential pitfalls, from low to high risk.

- Bank CDs are insured time deposits that have guaranteed rates of return, which usually are not very high.
- U.S. treasury bills are government-backed securities with maturities of three months, six months, or one year. (At maturity, the security is guaranteed to have a certain face value, more than you paid.) The minimum purchase is $10,000.
- U.S. treasury notes are intermediate-term securities, mature in one to ten years, and can be purchased with as little as $1,000 of face value, depending on the maturity length. (What you pay when you buy is less than face value, which is the value when you cash them in.)
- U.S. treasury bonds are long-term investments with maturities of 10 to 30 years and can be purchased with a face value of as little as $1,000. All Treasury securities can be purchased through banks and brokers, but the most economical way is to buy them *directly* from the Federal Reserve, 202-874-4000, through its Treasury Direct program. Also, by buying directly, the treasury pays you the interest *up front* instead of at maturity. Note that when treasury securities are redeemed *before* maturity, their value can't be assured, because of regular interest-rate changes. Generally, the returns from treasury securities are exempt from federal and state income taxes.

- Government savings bonds can be purchased in denominations of as little as $50, actually costing you only $25 at the time of purchase. Income taxes are deferred until redemption, the time of which varies according to interest rates.
- Government zero-coupon bonds operate in a similar manner but can require high commissions, and income taxes are not deferred but paid *before* receiving the interest.
- Government Series EE savings bonds, as mentioned in the previous chapter, are exempt from taxes under certain conditions when used for college tuition and fees.
- Mutual funds are registered investment companies that pool investor money to issue shares, each of which represents the value of shares of a broad variety of company stock, treasury securities, municipal bonds, corporate bonds, international stocks or bonds, real estate holdings, precious metals mining stocks, or a combination of any of these. Immediate diversification is created by this concept, so when you invest money in a mutual fund, your risk is spread and, therefore, reduced.

THE VALUE OF MUTUAL FUNDS

Mutual funds are an ideal investment because of their diversification, low minimum investment requirements, professional management that eliminates the need for you to research companies yourself, lack of a broker in most cases, no-load policies that are up-front sales charges or commissions, easily accessible price listings available in most daily newspapers, and the many highly convenient services available to shareholders. The treasury securities mentioned previously are available more conveniently through mutual funds with no maturity periods to be concerned with.

Mutual funds permit the nonwealthy to gain access to that which can create wealth, because of their low investing requirements. Now more than 7,000 mutual funds exist, many of which are regularly charted in detail and discussed in magazines such as *Money, Kiplingers' Personal Finance, Smart Money,* and others found in your public library.

Do so many options make it tough to narrow down your choice? Not really. Read the charts and check out one-year, five-year, and ten-year *average annual returns* after eliminating loaded funds and those that have high minimum-investment requirements. Knowing the long-term record of good returns says a lot. Generally, beware of funds that have been in existence only one or two years and have not had a chance to prove themselves.

Most mutual funds are in "families" under the management of one company. These families may consist of short- and long-term bond funds, tax-exempt bond funds, conservative to aggressive stock funds (aggressive meaning willing to take higher short-term risk for faster and higher long-term gains, producing greater volatility), international funds that invest primarily abroad, global funds that invest in domestic and foreign companies, pools of home mortgages, index funds that attempt to base themselves to a key stock market average, and a host of sector funds that invest in specific types of industries such as health care or technology.

Most fund families offer an array of free services to shareholders such as automatic investment plans in which you specify what day each month and how much money the fund can take from your bank account by electronic funds transfer (EFT), switching money from one fund in the family to another, redeeming shares, daily fund price and market quote recordings, and retirement plan services. Most of these services can be accomplished by telephone and some services can be performed over the Internet as well.

Once you have made your choice of possible funds to invest in, call their toll-free numbers to request prospectuses and applications. All fund companies are required to send prospectuses to new potential shareholders. The prospectus explains exactly how the fund operates, its history, required legal disclosures, and shareholder services.

HOW TO BENEFIT THE MOST
FROM MUTUAL FUNDS

Here are a few more tips that will help you obtain the greatest profit from investing in mutual funds:

- All mutual fund families have a money market fund that is useful as a cash reserve to park money until you have decided to invest it. These funds normally maintain a stable price per share of one dollar, investing in only the most conservative places such as government securities, and pay a nominal rate of interest comparable to a bank money market account. Though technically not insured, these funds are practically as secure as bank accounts.

- Most fund companies will open up accounts as IRAs, 403(b), 401(k), SEP, Keogh, and other IRS-qualified retirement plans, charging a nominal annual fee of $10 to $20 to maintain the account and waiving the fees when balances grow high, such as more than $10,000. The longer you invest, the more aggressively you might want to invest, because you can afford short-term price swings in share value for potentially spectacular long-term rewards. Because retirement money normally is invested for the long-term, such accounts are ideal places to invest very aggressively. One of the major downfalls of countless holders of retirement accounts is not investing in stock funds. The difference between account holders who leave their money in an account earning 4 percent per year instead of 14 percent could involve *hundreds of thousands* of dollars by retirement age.
- Mutual funds pay dividends every year based on how much buying and selling they do and dividends paid by the companies whose stock they invest in. You may elect to have these dividends paid to you in cash or reinvested as additional shares. If building your wealth remains your goal, reinvest the dividends to increase the rate of growth. Note that fund share prices drop by the amount of dividends paid out, while your net asset value (NAV), the cash value of all your shares, stays the same, giving you *more shares at a lower price.* Now with more shares working for you, when the share price rises, you will increase your net worth at a faster rate.
- Some funds buy and sell more frequently than others and/or invest in more companies that pay dividends, which increases the dividends those funds pay. This rate of dividend payout is called the *tax efficiency* of the fund, because dividends are taxable income unless in a retirement plan or tax-exempt fund. Investing in a fund that pays more in dividends *does not* necessarily mean you make more money, because more taxes must be paid and dividend-paying stocks may not rise in prices as fast as those that don't pay much in dividends.
- What types of funds should you invest in? This depends on your financial goals. For a monthly income flow, you may want to place more of your money in *bond funds.* Corporate bond funds, government bond funds, municipal bond funds, and tax-exempt bond funds can benefit those in higher tax brackets. While government bond funds are nearly risk-free, their interest rates are lower than most corporate bond funds. Beware that all bonds and

bond funds can fluctuate in price, some considerably, with changes in interest rates.

- If you are young and investing for a minimum of five years, stock funds have been known to have returns that double or triple those of bond funds, though I cannot guarantee such performance.
- If you're invested in stock funds for the long-term, as I have been for years, don't panic during a market crash such as the one in October of 1987. I saw the equivalent of two years of my work salary "vanish" in less than two hours at that time. However, I *made money* off that crash! I used the tax strategy of *selling* shares in some of my mutual funds and *buying* shares in others, which gave me heavy capital gains losses to deduct off my income taxes as well as the opportunity to buy shares at an incredibly low price. Within months, share prices went right back up, totally offsetting that drop, and have increased 100 percent to 300 percent since!

GENERAL INVESTMENT TIPS

Aside from mutual funds, many other investment techniques can greatly help reduce the risks of investing. Among them are the following:

- Keep in mind that as much as economic forces such as interest rates, government deficits, trade balances, employment rates, and other economic factors do affect the stock market, ultimately people continue to purchase products and services in ever greater amounts as the population grows, the demand for new technologies and higher standards of living increases, and investors want to invest and make money. With all these factors taken into account, the long-term trend for stock markets is *up*, even if riding a roller coaster to get there. Also, much of the market is driven by unwarranted psychological aspects that have dramatic short-term consequences.
- Dollar cost averaging is an investment strategy based on the assumption that an investor invests a fixed sum of money each month. During times when the share price is lower, this fixed sum buys more shares that, over several years, rewards the investor better than investing larger sums less often. This is a good strategy for the wage earner who has only a certain amount of extra cash available to invest each month.

Wisdom on Wealth

It has been proven, however, that *on the average* if one comes into a large sum of money, one's investing results will fare better if the *entire amount is invested in the stock market all at once*, even if the Dow Jones and other averages are at all-time highs.

- Don't try to time the market. Waiting with a big wad of cash in anticipation of a market slide or crash may be like waiting for rain in the desert. Jump in, be patient, and wait it out. Many of the best stock market pros have not been successful at timing. Look at price postings of funds on a regular basis more for amusement, but if a fund continually underperforms others in the same category, after six months to a year, seriously consider replacing it with another fund. Note that each time you sell or switch among funds a tax consequence is generated, so frequent transactions of this type can gradually create tax headaches later. Some funds charge fees after so many switches in the same year.
- If you know you're about to make a large purchase, such as a house or car, or have other major expenses and your fund has just experienced a major rise, sell what you need, because the likelihood of a fall in price is greater after a sudden large rise. Keep in mind the tax consequences of redeeming shares. Ways of minimizing income taxes when selling shares are referred to in the next chapter. Generally, you may want to sell those shares you paid the most for, creating the least amount of gain to report.
- To determine if it is a savings for you to invest in a tax-exempt investment, apply this simple formula. Take the yield of the investment as a percentage and multiply it by 1 minus your tax bracket percent. Then multiply this result by 100. For example, if you have a taxable bond yielding 7 percent and you are in the 28 percent tax bracket, multiply .07 × (1 − .28 or .72). This equals .0504, which when multiplied by 100 equals 5.04 percent. Your tax-exempt yield, therefore, must be more than 5.04 percent to be a worthwhile investment in your particular case.
- In addition to your tax bracket, your *age* is the other major factor when determining what type of investment to be in. As you age,

it is normally recommended to lower your risk with investing because you have fewer years left for the risk to pay off. This concept is sound and certainly one should be receiving more *dependable periodical income* on retirement. Because many people still live another 20+ years after retirement, however, the most profitable strategy may be to keep most of what money is not needed to produce an income flow invested more aggressively.

- What about investment newsletters? Many are well written and contain some good, updated advice. You can obtain a catalog of investment newsletters for free from Select Information Service at 212-247-6720. Many newsletters send out free samples.

OTHER INVESTMENT OPPORTUNITIES

Stocks

Should you invest in individual stocks? Sure, but unless you have some background in the technical aspects of how the market works and information about specific companies or wish to put in the time to learn, you may be better off letting your mutual fund managers do the job. Once you have several tens of thousands of dollars in mutual funds, however, branching out into some specific stocks may increase your wealth.

There are several methods of investing in stocks. There is the *full-service broker* who supposedly has the knowledge and experience to pick higher-returning stocks for a commission, *discount brokers* who buy stocks for you based on your recommendation, and various ways to *buy stock directly* from companies without any additional fee—perhaps even from your employer. Numerous excellent books on how to buy stock free of commissions through DRIPs (dividend reinvestment plans), etc., are also available. The most frustration inexperienced investors may have is in realizing that by the time inside information about companies is published, it is likely to be outdated. For busy, working people who don't have time to research companies, the simplicity of investing in well-managed mutual funds can't be beat.

Real Estate

Some investors won't get near the stock market and instead create substantial wealth investing in real estate. Typically, real estate investors have made much of their money using the principle of *leverage*, that of controlling considerable assets with very little money. For example, if you can put down just $2,000 for a $100,000 house and have it appreciate 4 percent the first year, you will have made a 100 percent return on your $2,000 investment. In theory this concept is ideal, but finding dependable and responsible renters, keeping maintenance costs low, and maintaining rental income that allows you to break even on your mortgage and taxes may not be so simple.

Another way to earn dollars from real estate is for the *rental income to exceed* your monthly mortgage, taxes, insurance, and maintenance costs. For those who hold property for the long-term and keep it rented, they can make out well, especially when the mortgage is paid off.

And the third way to successfully invest in real estate is to buy property that needs work, in a good neighborhood. Certain houses can be bought for less than half of what other houses sell for, if you are handy, willing to sweat, and have the time to do major repairs. I have known people who have spent about $5,000 on building materials and paint and within a few months were able to sell a home they purchased for under $50,000 for more than $75,000. The easiest way to find such properties is by driving around and looking for them. The first obvious sign of these properties is the one- to two-foot-tall grass.

Other ways to locate potential real estate opportunities are:

- Look for bankruptcies, divorce records, lawsuits and liens, evictions, drug busts, or other legal matters that leave an individual or taxing authority in great need to sell. Your county courthouse, newspaper classifieds, and some REALTORS® can be good resources.
- Governmental agencies occasionally hold *real estate auctions*, another way to purchase property at bargain prices.
- If you are able to get good financing or have the cash, *purchasing discounted mortgages* from those who need cash can be rewarding. Check your local county deeds office and newspaper classifieds.
- Depending on the circumstance, assuming an existing mortgage can be a buyer's opportunity.

COLLECTIBLES

Can you be the one who finds a $2 million van Gogh for $5 at a garage sale? Probably not. For most items such as coins, stamps, jewelry, comic books, and antiques, unless you are a dealer or well seasoned in the business, you will pay a *retail* price for these things yet only be able to sell for *wholesale*.

GOLD

Though gold has been a standby for thousands of years and is still considered a hedge against economic catastrophe by many investors, I don't recommend keeping more than 10 percent of your portfolio in gold. If you're going to invest in gold, buy gold mining company stock or mutual funds that invest only in mining stocks rather than storing the metal in your home or renting a safe deposit box. The increase in value of stock shares will be worth more than corresponding gold price increases without the risk of holding onto the metal yourself.

INVESTING YOUR MONEY IN RETIREMENT PLANS

Depending on how much you earn and what benefits your employer offers, you may have a variety of *great opportunities* in retirement plans. The most common are individual retirement accounts (IRAs), 401(k)s, simplified employee pensions (SEPs), 403(b)s, Keoghs, and Defined Benefit Plans. Of course, wage earners will be eligible to collect Social Security, as well, if they have built up enough work credits to qualify. If you want to continue to live comfortably and treat yourself to a few of the finer things in life, however, you will need more income than Social Security will provide. Most financial advisers estimate it will cost you about 70 percent of your previous wages to live after retiring, though many live in style on far less.

The IRA serves as a great vehicle for many to save money on taxes, as well as defer taxes on all interest, dividends, and capital gains. Several rules apply to obtain the maximum benefits. For those who earn at least $2,000 in a year but not more than about $25,000, if single, or about $40,000, if married (both figures are altered for inflation regularly), they can exclude up to $2,000, if single, and $4,000, if married, from their income by placing these funds into an IRA account and receive the added benefit of tax deferral, as long as the funds stay in the account. Even a nonworking spouse can take a $2,000 IRA deduction off a working spouse's wages. Those who earn more than the income thresholds can still place these amounts into an IRA, but only on a nondeductible basis, still get the tax deferral benefit, and pay no taxes at withdrawal time. Keogh plans permit self-employed persons to stash away more tax-deferred money than an IRA, but employers must usually provide the plan to employees as well.

SEPs and 401(k)s are offered primarily by employers of for-profit corporations that choose to participate in such plans. The more generous ones match employee contributions up to a certain percentage, an excellent offer all employees should participate in. In most cases, the amount you choose to contribute to these plans is deducted directly from your paycheck untaxed. The IRS now allows almost $10,000 a year to be placed in 401(k) plans and $30,000 into SEPs, subject to percentages of wages. The government is currently considering ways to help boost savings, so these caps may soon be extended. Even employer contributions are untaxed.

The 403(b) plans are similar to other retirement plans, but they are primarily for employees of nonprofit and public educational institutions. All retirement plans require you to not withdraw funds for more than a 60-day period in a given year until at least the age of 59½ to avoid a 10 percent early withdrawal penalty. Also, amounts withdrawn become taxable income for that year, if untaxed when deposited. There are exceptions for extreme hardship, such as disability. Congress is also considering changes that would permit tax-free or penalty-free withdrawals for down payments on a first house or for a child's college education.

WITHDRAWING MONEY AND PENALTIES

With many retirement plans, you can choose where to invest your money. From stocks, bonds, mutual funds, precious metals, and real estate to bank CDs, placing your money in the right investment vehicles can pay off handsomely! Most retirement plans have "custodians" who manage the account and charge management fees from zero to more than $100 a year. If you are being charged more than $25 a year, go shopping for other places to invest your money. Never use a custodian who charges fees based on a percentage of the account's value.

When your account is valued at $100,000 even a quarter of a percent equals $250!

Direct transfers of funds from one custodial institution to another are simple to make and involve no tax consequences. But *withdrawing* involves rules you should be very aware of:

- A rollover allows you to move funds from one qualifying retirement plan to another. You must instruct the custodian to send the money directly to the new custodian you have made arrangements with, or if a custodian sends a check to you, have it made out to the new custodian.
- Don't place IRA withdrawals in your name when transferring them to new custodians. A major tax penalty of 20 percent is imposed and withheld immediately, though it can be refunded when filing your taxes.
- Don't hold any funds you have received in your name from retirement accounts for more than 60 days or an additional 10 percent penalty will be imposed if you are under the age of 59½. Some states assess early withdrawal penalties as well.
- The IRS imposes a 6 percent penalty for excess contributions in a given year and continues to charge this amount each year until the excess is withdrawn.
- You can avoid the 10 percent early withdrawal penalty if: (1) you are disabled to the extent that you are unemployable as defined by federal tax law, (2) you withdraw all or a portion of your current year contribution before the extended deadline for tax filing for the same year plus dividends or interest, (3) you receive a distribution as the beneficiary of someone's IRA after his or her death, or (4) you annuitize distributions in "substantially equal periodic payments" based on your life expectancy or the combined life expectancy of you and your beneficiary, subject to early withdrawal penalties if altered before you reach the age of 59½ or five years, whichever is later.
- By April 1 following the year in which you reach the age of 70½, the IRS requires you to begin withdrawing a minimum amount from your IRA as defined by life-expectancy formulas.
- Unlike a 401(k), you can't borrow from an IRA or use it as a pledge for a loan.
- IRAs may be canceled and refunded from custodians if written notice is received or postmarked within seven days of opening the account.

- You have the right to change your beneficiary designations at any time, though keep in mind that choosing a beneficiary many years younger than you to decrease withdrawal amounts will only work for those up to ten years younger. So it won't work for grandpa to combine his life expectancy with his two-year-old granddaughter.

Many employer plans will only permit you to invest in *the employer's* stock and/or one or two other sources, which usually are conservative for long-term investing. Many workers start and are contributing to retirement plans from as early as their 20s into their 60s. In the majority of circumstances, therefore, retirement money is being invested for 10 to more than 40 years, giving it lots of time to compound, the *ideal breeding ground for aggressive growth* investments. As already alluded to, the longer you invest, the more risk diminishes and the better chance you have of receiving *much higher* annual average returns. Just keep in mind that an account worth $2,000,000 could fluctuate in value by $35,000 a *day* in aggressive investments or more than $100,000 in less than a year. Thus, when you come within a few years of withdrawing retirement money, it may be wise to place some of it into more conservative *income-producing* investments.

Wisdom on Wealth

In the majority of circumstances, therefore, retirement money is being invested for 10 to more than 40 years, giving it lots of time to compound, the *ideal breeding ground for aggressive growth* investments.

WHERE NOT TO INVEST

The Federal Bureau of Investigation (FBI) estimates that con artists bilk more than $200 billion each year from people of all levels and backgrounds—the rich, poor, educated and uneducated, young, old, men, women, and all races. Clever swindlers can fool virtually *anyone.* They usually communicate in polite and charming manners with great enthusiasm about some grand opportunity.

The worst "investments" are not real investments at all, but scams. The first indications of fraud often appear in the form of highly sensational advertising in newspapers, magazines, junk mail, or a telephone call that promises to multiply your money by severalfold over a short period of time. Here are some actual quotes I have observed from such hype:

- "No selling or phoning."
- "Have at least $500 in your pocket in 24 hours for only minutes of your time."
- "No end to the cash flow."
- "Your living room will soon look like the U.S. Mint."
- "Earn $10,000 to $20,000 a month."

Quotes such as these should immediately signal trouble. Some "guarantee" returns of 15 percent to 30 percent or more per year, which is not realistic for *any* investment. Others promise you the moon if you are gullible enough to believe it. Worst of all, prosecution of swindlers does not happen very often and when it does, penalties are not usually stiff enough to deter such behavior. Someone has to be a big-time money-laundering drug trafficker to get more jail time for writing a hot check for $20 than devastating the financial lives of a thousand people. Increased awareness and prevention are the most effective approaches in dealing with white-collar crime. The following is a list of common scams to watch out for:

- The Ponzi or pyramid scheme: Money is collected from new investors merely to pay off previous investors' high returns, until the scheme collapses, goes bankrupt, and leaves the remaining investors robbed of their money. Usually no tangible assets are actually invested in.
- Get-rich-quick manuals: Books full of questionable ways to make big money fast, the sales of which may weigh down the pockets of their authors while lightening the buyers' pockets.
- Telemarketing fraud: Being promised goods or a winning prize by telephone for an up-front fee and never seeing the goods or prize. Being billed 900-number charges for worthless services or those that are offered for free somewhere else. Having your long-distance carrier switched without your authorization. There are more.

- Advertisements in newspapers and magazines saying you can earn high figures by stuffing envelopes, watching TV, or assembling things.
- Stockbrokers who trade your stock portfolio too frequently, known as "churning." Each buy-or-sell trade generates commission income for brokers. Proving they are churning and pursuing it in court is not easy, so if you suspect this is taking place, fire the broker.
- Loans that are actually second mortgages on your home: A salesperson comes to your home and tricks you into signing your house away.
- Letting others use your good credit history in return for cash that can obligate you for an enormous sum many times more than the quick cash. As cited by Ken and Daria Dolan in *Money* magazine, May, 1996, this scheme occurs when you qualify for a loan and transfer this obligation to someone else who pays you a fee. After you are paid about $1,000 in cash for this service, this "someone else" may leave you on the hook for the entire loan balance of far more than $1,000.
- Social Security information for a fee: Getting new SS cards for children, earnings records, and eligibility information are all free services provided by Social Security directly.
- Banking and credit-card fraud: This happens when swindlers get and use your credit-card numbers, bank-account numbers, and Social Security numbers. Keep these numbers private.
- Lists of "great" job opportunities: The ads for these lists sound wonderful, but the jobs may require outrageous and/or obscure skills or be in far less than adequate conditions.
- Government surplus giveaways: Claims that the government is selling expensive new cars for under $500 from drug busts and similar claims. When pursued, the claims have major hitches or don't exist.
- Online scams in which stock and/or commodity prices are hyped, causing their price to shoot up to artificially high levels.
- Weight loss and medical scams: Outrageous claims of diet supplements and miracle cures by purchasing overpriced, worthless, and sometimes even dangerous substances, as cited in the May 15, 1990, issue of *Family Circle* magazine.

- Schemes involving the exchanging of money in which no product or service is provided: These offer advice on how to go about making money the same way their ads said. Usually name and address lists are circulated just to keep money flowing and nothing else.

MULTILEVEL SALES

Lots of companies engage in multilevel or network marketing. Their major effort, after selling what they offer, is recruiting more salespeople. This is understandable for these companies use only independent salespeople to sell their products. Often new recruits are customers themselves or referrals from them. In most cases new salespeople are expected or required to purchase the products or services being offered. Network marketing companies offer weight-loss products, mineral and vitamin supplements, household and cleaning agents, energy-saving devices, insurance and mutual funds, gifts, health foods, cosmetics, and more. Often there is an initial investment of up to $500 to get started, some or all of which may be reimbursed by recruiting new people and generating sales. Many salespeople only end up breaking even with their investment, some make marginal incomes, while a few make high incomes from working long hours, having the right personality to sell and recruit, and convincing friends, relatives, and coworkers to buy products and offer their homes for demonstrations. Once you establish a sales force, you may be paid well from override commissions. Unless you are highly determined to be successful in network marketing or can make use of these products or services economically, your time and money may be put to better use.

GETTING HELP

In any of these money-making "opportunities," if you intend to make an investment, no matter how small, it is wise to use the following agencies to receive and report information:

- The Better Business Bureau: The BBB will tell you how many, if, and what types of complaints have been filed against the business in question and assist in resolving an existing complaint you have. Not having complaints on file does not confirm that the

business is now conducting its affairs properly. Some BBBs
charge small fees for their services.

- Ask a trustworthy friend who has used the business. Good referrals are a free, valuable resource.
- Contact your state attorney general's office. Its consumer-affairs
department can assist you and handle complaints, and it has legal
authority.
- State securities boards: They handle information, complaints,
licensing requirements, and legal pursuits of companies dealing
in stocks, bonds, mortgage notes, oil and gas leases, and more.

Four helpful agencies to call are: The National Fraud Information
Bureau, 800-876-7060; Call For Action, 202-537-0585; the Direct Selling
Association, 202-293-5760; and the Securities and Exchange Commission (broker problems), 800-732-0330. All are very helpful and can
direct you to the right source if they can't help.

At this point you should have a clear understanding of the difference
between *saving* and *investing,* with the latter depending on the former. I
know many people I commend for their excellent ability to customize
their lifestyle in such a manner to have saved amazing sums for their
income. However, when I ask *where* they leave their savings and am
told, "in a savings account," a red flag goes up, realizing that they could
be adding substantially more to their wealth-building results by investing their savings with minimal risk. With self-discipline and the knowledge presented in this chapter, you should be on the road to financial
freedom in the not-too-distant future.

Wisdom on Wealth

It is essential to feel comfortable with some
level of risk. Most financial achievements are
accomplished through disciplined savings and
calculated risk.

CHAPTER 12

Minimizing Your
Tax Burden

Keeping your taxes to a minimum is another essential method of maintaining your level of wealth rising at the fastest possible rate. There is no good reason to pay a dollar more in taxes than is required. In this chapter you will find the most important tax-saving methods that apply to the majority of people. No financial plan is complete without using the tax system to its advantage.

Wisdom on Wealth

There is no good reason to pay a dollar more in taxes than is required.

Three major forms of taxes you can't completely avoid, at least not legally, are *property*, *sales*, and *income taxes*. Whether you own or rent property, you are paying taxes on it. Some think that property taxes should be banned because they believe the purchase of real estate should operate just like buying a couch or a TV, without further financial obligations. These people even question if individuals ever really own property as long as another entity has the right to take it away. On the other side of this issue is the clear fact that money for police and fire protection, road repair, public schools, street lighting, and trash pickup must come from somewhere. If not from property taxes then get ready for higher income taxes, sales taxes, user fees, or some other enforceable method of extracting money from your pockets.

With sales taxes you have little choice because you must pay taxes at the time of purchase, the exceptions being sales from newspaper ads, garage sales, and bartering. Ordering products by mail used to allow you to avoid sales taxes in some cases, but then there are shipping and handling charges. It is worth comparing your cost of buying locally. Several states recently are litigating to enforce companies that are out of state to pay in-state sales taxes, so this advantage may be one that is on its way out.

Two basic types of income taxes are payable in most places: state taxes and the federal income tax that you pay to the IRS. Some places also impose local income taxes collected by a city or county. Not many states are left without an income tax and those that don't have one often compensate by having higher sales and/or property taxes. Each area differs in its tax rates and rules that can significantly affect your cost of living.

THE INTERNAL REVENUE SERVICE

It is the IRS that many people dread dealing with, whether it be resentment toward the nearly limitless power the IRS has to enforce the collection of taxes, the amount of taxes, how taxes are spent, or the inequality of the tax code.

The IRS has always been given broad authority over the citizens of the United States by legislators to ensure the ability of the government to operate. This situation is not likely to change. Just as with a hornet hive, however, if you deal with the IRS appropriately, then you will have little to fear. Here are a few suggestions:

- Three words keep your dealings with the IRS smooth and easy. These are *knowledge, honesty,* and *proof.*
- Pay the least amount of tax you can, but have an *orderly record* of exactly why you are able to do so.
- *Learn and fully understand all tax rules* that relate to each entry and changes you make on tax forms and keep copies of these rules with copies of your forms for five years.

- Keep each year's tax filing information and forms in a *separate envelope* or *folder* marked by the year for simplicity, in the event that you are questioned.
- If you don't understand a tax rule as it may apply to your situation, *don't make assumptions!* Call 800-829-1040, visit the IRS office near you, get free advice from tax volunteers who meet people in public libraries, or hire a tax professional.

Wisdom on Wealth

Three words keep your dealings with the IRS smooth and easy. These are *knowledge, honesty,* and *proof.*

It is human nature to want to accumulate wealth for oneself and some people try to cut corners to do so. When the IRS finds out that tax cheating is taking place, however, the consequences are *not pleasant.* Cheating can carry not only a fine plus back taxes, interest, and penalties, but a jail term as well. In serious matters, the IRS can seize your assets and garnish your wages. With all the legal tax breaks and money-saving strategies presented here, you don't need to walk on thin ice with the IRS.

Regardless of every effort made by taxpayers to be honest, there are several reasons why they can be audited:

- Random Taxpayer Compliance Measurement Program (TCMP) audits anyone. These thorough audits are performed for IRS statistical purposes to find out how best to improve other auditing techniques.
- Known criminals have the highest chance of being audited and professional self-employed people with incomes of more than $50,000 a year come in second.
- Lower tax bracket earners with incomes from $10,000 to $30,000 a year only have a 2 percent chance of being audited in a given year.
- Others are audited because their finances are too extreme for the statistical norm. For example, if a taxpayer earns only $12,000 a year but has more than $10,000 in deductions, or unearned income that dramatically increases from one year to the next, this may arouse curiosity.

- From April 15, the due date for most tax returns, the IRS has three years to challenge your return or, if late, the date your return is postmarked. If the IRS can determine that you have *intentionally understated* taxes due or other clear marks of fraud, the statute has *no limit*. In most cases, where no willful behavior on the part of the taxpayer to avoid taxes is indicated, the IRS is not permitted to audit the same parts of your return within three years after an audit.

Many audits are activated because of IRS errors. Some errors are of mammoth proportions and others minor, but if you have all necessary documentation, your major concern may not be having to pay more taxes, but dealing with the IRS bureaucracy. Solving even minor problems that are not your fault can take months. In some cases it is necessary to consult an attorney, especially if the IRS is threatening to seize your property or you just have complex matters to handle.

Normally, your first notice of an audit will arrive as a computer-generated letter. You may respond—always by certified mail—and cause the audit to be delayed because the law says that the time and place of the meeting must be convenient to each party. Simply let the IRS know a good time to meet that will give you time to get all your documentation in order and consult a CPA or lawyer, if needed. Note, however, that if you owe taxes, interest will keep accumulating on your tax debt with each passing day, so act fast. If your audit notice is not specific enough, you have the right to ask just what details of your tax situation are in question. Some problems can be resolved by telephone or mail.

BEHAVE YOURSELF

Even if you are 100 percent confident that you are correct and have a neat file of papers to prove it, beware of the following:

- Don't show signs of irritation *or* defensiveness. Stay calm.
- Hostility can be construed by auditors as behavior in which taxpayers are trying to cover up something, even though you may only be angry that you had to leave work for an afternoon and drive 20 miles.
- Don't volunteer more information than the auditor requests.
- Pleading ignorance, misinterpretation of a tax rule, being disorganized, or being a tax protester will not score points, most of the time.

- When you are highly confident of your opinion, speak up and say so.

If you are having trouble resolving an issue with the IRS, start moving up the chain of command. My auditor told me, "I have discussed your case with my supervisor" as a technique to keep me from bothering to go over his head. I had a perfect right to, as everyone does. If supervisors don't help to your satisfaction, you may contact the Problem Resolution Office or the IRS Appeals Office, which are set up to lessen the burden of the tax courts. If all else fails, you can go to small-claims tax court where most decisions are final.

USE THE SYSTEM WISELY

Singles without dependents who have very little unearned income, and don't itemize their deductions, can file form 1040-EZ and have it completed in a few minutes. Only the most basic calculations are involved. If you have one or more dependents, use form 1040A, which will permit you to claim exemptions for dependents, as well as obtain a significant tax credit for child- and dependent-care expenses, and possibly be eligible for an earned income tax credit (EITC). As your income decreases you will get a greater percentage deducted, up to more than $1,000. This credit may equal more than whatever taxes you had withheld, yet you can still keep this full amount. Being able to receive more back from the IRS than you have withheld is a very rare exception. If you can be certain of being eligible in advance for this credit, then you may arrange with your employer to have less withheld from your paycheck in the present. Doing so gives you more cash to use in the present instead of giving the IRS an interest-free loan. Note that this principle applies to all W-4 withholding.

Wisdom on Wealth

Your target should be to owe the IRS nothing beyond what you have withheld from your employer and to get no refund either, though rarely is it possible to reach this goal exactly.

Sadly, I know someone with a family who is making a very poor choice to file form 1040-EZ year after year. With the family adjusted gross income of only about $22,000 a year, my acquaintance would be eligible for hundreds of dollars in earned income tax credit, hundreds of dollars more in personal exemptions for dependents (two live-in parents), hundreds more in child-care expense credits, hundreds more in IRA deductions, hundreds more in making appropriate adjustments to their employer withholding W-4 form, and more by itemizing on Schedule A. My acquaintance believes it is too time-consuming to file the longer form 1040 needed to take these allowable deductions. I figured his time to do so would be worth about *$500 an hour!* Even more sad, he and his wife often complain that they are just barely making it each month and can't fulfill their dreams. The combined figure for those who pay more taxes than they are required to adds up to a staggering sum.

DON'T BE AFRAID OF LONG FORMS

As you age and perhaps buy real estate, raise a family, start investing, and maybe own a business, you will certainly need to file the standard long form 1040. This is far more time-consuming, but worth the effort. As with the 1040A you will be able to claim exemptions for dependents, child-care expense credits, and earned income tax credit, if applicable. As your income rises, these deductions decrease and sometimes disappear completely. At around $100,000 to $150,000 of income per year, even personal exemptions are phased out.

As an extension of the 1040, the IRS has an elaborate system of forms and schedules to cover a multitude of possible tax circumstances taxpayers end up in. If all the IRS paperwork were placed together, including the instruction booklets, you would need a shelf 40 feet long. Fortunately, most taxpayers need only make use of less than a half-inch stack. Having access to this much information, however, is an opportunity for taxpayers for it permits them to learn numerous possible methods of using the system to their benefit. Those people who are well-educated on income taxes see filing taxes as more of a creative project than a time to be dreaded.

IRS SCHEDULE A

Schedule A is a tax form on which one lists *itemized deductions*, which must add up to more than the standard deduction on line 34 of the 1040 form. These deductions require proper documentation, normally both a receipt and a canceled check. As of 1995, depending on your marital status, you could take as much as $6,550 for a standard deduction. (Sadly, the IRS continues to penalize marriage, with most married couples paying from a few hundred to several thousand dollars a year more in federal taxes than if they were single.) These figures are adjusted up for inflation annually. Being as generous as they are, it permits many people to save time by not having to fill out Schedule A.

Sometimes, however, reviewing your deductions and filling out the Schedule A form can save you a lot of money. For starters, remember that when listing deductible expenses, you must have proper documentation, normally *both* a receipt and a canceled check. The following is a list of possible deductions:

- Homeowners can deduct all mortgage interest, property taxes, home equity loans and some home purchasing costs, such as points.
- You can deduct unreimbursed medical and dental costs that exceed 7.5 percent of adjusted gross income, including insurance premiums (reduced by any self-employed health insurance deduction), copayments, costs not covered by insurance, prescriptions, nursing help, eyeglasses, contact lenses, hearing aids, crutches, and wheelchairs. Hopefully, the 7.5 percent threshold will be lowered to make these deductions more useful. Note that if you are married and one of you can claim a greater dollar amount beyond this 7.5 percent, you may come out ahead by filing married separate rather than joint.
- Gifts to charity and certain expenses incurred volunteering for charity such as mileage are also deductible, subject to more detailed documentation if more than $250. Keep detailed information about how you determined the value of items donated to charity other than cash.
- Theft and casualty losses not covered by insurance are deductible with the exception of misplaced property or cash, damaged property under normal conditions, and progressive damage to property such as termites or the natural deterioration of a roof.

- Unreimbursed employee expenses such as noncommuting job travel, union dues, job education, required uniforms, tools, tax preparation fees, and custodial account fees (including IRAs) are deductible for totals that exceed 2 percent of your adjusted gross income.
- Gambling losses to the extent of winnings are deductible.
- Various management costs incurred in overseeing any revenue-generating property, if not deducted elsewhere, are eligible as deductions.

If your total of all deductions from Schedule A is greater than your standard deduction, use the former amount in place of the standard deduction. If not, you have not wasted your time completely, for you have learned how many deductions you have and what you can do to generate more next year.

Wisdom on Wealth

One smart technique when trying to beat the standard deduction is to bunch your expenses together as much as possible by expediting or delaying expenses that would otherwise not fall within the same tax year.

OTHER DEDUCTIONS

If you have children and are paying for child-care, after-school care, and baby-sitting, file Form 2441 that permits parents to get a dependent-care credit of up to several hundred dollars per child.

If you are considered disabled on a long-term basis so that you cannot engage in "substantial gainful activity," you are likely to qualify for tax credits. A doctor will have to verify your condition on Schedule R, although you will have to file this form only once. Tax credits are available from under $100 to more than $1,000, depending on other needs you may have, your marital status, and your age.

A number of expenses related to moving are deductible on Form 3903. First of all "your move must be closely related, both in time and in place, to the start of work at your new job location" and "your new main job location must be at least 50 miles farther from your former home than your old main job location," according to IRS Publication 17. Anyone with even mildly complex taxes should order Publication 17 by calling 800-TAX-FORM. Also you are required to work at least 39 weeks full-time during the first 12 months at your new location, though not necessarily consecutively or for the same employer. Self-employed people are expected to work 78 weeks after a move. You can deduct the cost of packing, transporting all household goods yourself or by a moving company, storage and insurance for up to 30 days, utility reconnect fees, and lodging expenses based on a direct route. Meals are not deductible.

Are you over the age of 65? A couple of things that seniors must be aware of are the additional exemption that may be claimed if they are 65 or older, only paying taxes on taxable income, and filing quarterly as needed to avoid end-of-the-year penalties. Many list their Social Security benefits in full as income, as well as income from tax-free bonds, while only a small portion of it may be taxable.

SCHEDULES B AND D

Bank interest, dividends, and capital gains and losses must be reported in your taxes. In recent years, any dividends and interest that exceed $400 require the filing of Schedule B. Any capital gains and losses from the sale of stocks, bonds, mutual funds, precious metals, real estate, collectibles, cars, and certain other items are reported on Schedule D. Generally, you must record the date of a purchase, what you paid for the item, the date the item was sold, its selling price, and the difference in dollars between the time of purchase and the time of sale. If the difference is a gain or loss, record it as such. There are short-term gains and long-term gains (held over one year) that fall under different categories on your forms; long-term are normally favored over short-term.

When it comes to your taxes, those who have taken advantage of dollar cost averaging with their mutual funds can benefit from substantial savings on their returns. After several years, you are more likely to have purchased shares at so many different prices that you may be in a better position to create both losses and gains, which can offset each other—up to a point. Just keep track of which shares you have sold, so you don't accidentally report selling the same shares again, which would not increase your popularity with the IRS.

CALCULATING INVESTMENT GAINS

Several methods are available to calculate investment gains, some of which can be hair-wrenching. Some mutual funds will automatically average your cost basis when you sell, which is convenient, though not always the most cost-effective. What you want to do is pick those shares with the highest cost to decrease your taxable gain or, better yet, create losses.

Another method is the first in, first out method (FIFO), which means those shares purchased first must be those sold first. Whatever method you use, the IRS requires you to continue using the same method for the duration of your ownership of the fund. The IRS permits up to $3,000 of losses in a year to cancel out gains and lets taxpayers continue to write off losses against gains for losses over $3,000 in a given year, for up to ten years.

Another strategy that was mentioned in the investment chapter is to "trade" shares from one investment to another immediately after a sudden, major drop to generate more losses. I tell people that if they must get cash from their mutual funds, to limit their need to what they pay in dividends instead of having them reinvested, to create less tax consequences. Also, if investing a lump sum, it can be tax wise to invest it just after a fund declares dividends to avoid further tax liability, if within a couple of months of dividend payouts. This way you won't be paying taxes on additional shares just purchased.

TAXES AND REAL ESTATE

A long chapter could be devoted to this complex topic. Plenty of updated income tax guides are available in bookstores and, of course, free publications from the IRS, which I recommend reading carefully for more details than I can provide in this book. Here are a few suggestions:

- Deduct points and other costs associated with closings, as well as property taxes paid each year.
- *Save all receipts* that prove you paid for permanent additions, structural improvements, repairs, and replacement of major appliances. Most of these costs can be subtracted from the gain when you sell your house.

- Rental and royalty income must be reported on Schedule E but is able to be offset by a variety of deductible expenses and depreciation costs.
- To keep money in the family and increase the likelihood of fair rent, consider renting to and from other family members. Children who buy their parents' house and then rent it back to them, can take advantage of a substantial tax savings, in addition to the other benefits. Immediate family are more likely to pay their rent on time and take care of their residence. I am assuming that relatives are on excellent terms to engage in such major financial commitments.
- If you're at least 55 years old, the IRS will allow you to take a once-in-a-lifetime exclusion of $125,000 on the gain of the sale of a residence.
- Others may defer whatever part of the gain is used to purchase another property within the replacement period as specified by the IRS. Presently, the replacement period is two years from when the gain is realized. The problem here is that buying a more expensive house may go against the philosophy of living on less. File Schedule E and Forms 2119 and 4562 when dealing with real estate transactions.
- If you get heavily involved in managing investment properties, and your taxes become more complex, weigh the value of spending your time filing your own taxes versus hiring a tax professional.

YOUR OWN BUSINESS

Filing business tax forms can be even more complicated and exhausting than the ones for investment properties. By the time you get through Schedule C, Form 2106, and 4265 you may have wished you'd hired a tax preparer instead (note that your best bet when hiring tax assistance is by using "enrolled agents," those employed by the IRS for at least five years and having passed a rigorous two-day exam). A long list of expenses associated with owning a business are deductible or at least may become deductible once they depreciate. Here are a few:

- Use part or all of your residence for operating your business, if appropriate.

- Employ your own spouse and children in your business, paying them and providing benefits in tax-deductible dollars.
- Children under the age of 19 can earn about $4,000 a year without even having to file taxes, as long as their investment income does not exceed $650.
- When they earn income, children are immediately eligible to open an IRA. With no minimum initial investment, it's a good idea to open an IRA for your child as soon as possible, so that compound interest will work to your child's greatest advantage. Even very young children can clean the office, stamp and seal envelopes, or perform some other basic tasks. A child would only have to work less than 15 hours a week at $6 an hour to easily reach the limit of nontaxable earned income. You can employ *your own* children under the age of 14 in this manner without conflicting with child-labor laws, while at the age of 14 they may work part-time for others. You must be able to document employment just as you would if hiring an adult.
- When you employ your child, you are getting a *quintuple* tax benefit: The child's wages and benefits are a business deduction, you don't have to pay federal unemployment taxes, whatever wages placed in an IRA create another deduction, you may still claim the child as a dependent exemption, and as long as your child is under the age of 19 you won't have to withhold Social Security taxes. There is no lower limit for hiring your own child if he or she is able to reasonably perform work assigned. Nearly newborn babies have been employed as models and earned enough to max out eligible retirement plan contributions!
- Deduct costs of personal items such as your car, computer, VCR, rent or mortgage, telephone, etc., on a partial basis, depending on how much they are used for business. Even vacations can be deducted to the extent they are used for business or applying for work. Document these types of deductions carefully.

CHILD SUPPORT

Another complex area that has many tax consequences is that of receiving and paying alimony and child support. It is crucial that you have these areas carefully detailed in your divorce decree. In most cases, the one *paying* alimony may deduct this expense and the one *receiving* it must pay taxes on it. Child-support expenses are not deductible.

TAXES AND YOUR RETIREMENT FUNDS

Generally, the more money you place in tax-deferred investments, the better, because for tax-free compounding will outweigh early withdrawal penalties over time. Many people with 403(b) and 401(k) plans also qualify for a deductible IRA, depending on gross income and how much is put into other tax-deferred plans. Beware that one can overdose on packing away everything "for the future," so if your income is more modest, invest a fair amount outside of retirement plans.

Wisdom on Wealth

Saving money until you are too old to enjoy it is self-defeating.

Another method many use to reap tax benefits is to tie up money in life insurance and annuities. Except for the wealthy, I don't recommend this approach to retirement planning. First of all, the only way you can profit from life insurance is to die young or soon after the inception of the policy. I feel the deepest regret for those who think saving taxes is worth *dying* for! Annuities are usually managed by life insurance companies and are set up to provide a guaranteed minimum level of income each month for a set number of years or for life. Their rate of return is not very high, but you get solid income security, which can be comforting in one's later years, despite the fact that you can hardly break even with inflation. Contributions to annuities and income from them is sheltered from taxes. As with other retirement plans, when you reach 70½, you are required to start withdrawing this money and may be eligible for "forward income averaging." Remember that an annuity is only as secure as the financial condition of the company offering it, so check out the rating of your annuity company before investing. Another reason the tax advantages of annuities must be substantial is that companies charge a lot to handle them. There are mortality fees, investment fees, and administration fees that can cut heavily into returns. Annuities go directly to beneficiaries and avoid probate in the event of death.

TRUSTS AND TAXES

Trust accounts are another way funds can be "locked up" for long periods of time with lower tax consequences. Many types of trusts exist and their complexity often requires the assistance of a lawyer to set them up. A financial institution must manage trust accounts and usually charges hefty fees for doing so.

The two major types of trusts are the revocable and irrevocable. Revocable means that the one who placed funds in the account continues to have control over it, while an irrevocable one is essentially a gift to be received at a specified time in the future. This is how numerous people leave funds for their children's future. You can specify how many years the account is untouchable and what exceptions may apply. Many, rightfully so, are concerned that when their children suddenly get this money, it may not be spent or invested wisely. This is why you may want to include stipulations in the trust and preferably have some control over it. You may want to have a trust for children that pays out its value or only interest over many years to keep children from getting an enormous windfall all at once. Doing so saves on taxes as well.

Trust accounts are required by the IRS to pay the 15 percent tax rate on approximately the first $3,500 of income, which is an advantage. With one exception, I recommend only wealthier people use trusts if management and legal fees are high. This exception is the Twentieth Century Gift Trust, 800-345-2021, which has a low minimum investment of only $250 and very modest management fees. This aggressive stock mutual fund has had stunning returns, averaging *around 25% annually* for many years! You are required to set the withdrawal time for a minimum of ten years into the future.

Another, easier way to put away funds for a child's future is to make use of the Uniform Gifts to Minors Act that permits parents or anyone to put money into an account for this purpose. The obvious tax benefit is that the first $650 (indexed up by $50 a year recently) of interest, dividends, or capital gains is tax-exempt every year, until a child reaches the age of 14. The next $650 of investment income is taxed at the child's lower rate, which most likely is 15 percent. Income beyond this level is taxed at the custodian's rate, normally a parent. After the child reaches the age of 14, investment income is taxed at whatever the child's rate is, and at age 18 to 21, depending on your state laws, the child can legally gain access to the funds. The IRS says that money placed into child custodial accounts must be used for expenses for the child, so when withdrawals are made, keep records of how the money was spent. Indirectly, this permits parents to spend less while saving on taxes.

CASH GIFTS

Remember that as parents, you each can give up to $10,000 per year to a child before having to pay the gift tax. This is a great way to keep wealth in the family, see your children enjoy the benefits of receiving some early inheritance while you're still living, and assure that some outrageously overcharging nursing home or other health-care establishment won't dry up everything you have spent your life working for. You are number one, however, *not your children*, so do this only after you are *sure* your finances are well set. Your children have their entire lifetimes ahead of them to work and build wealth.

Nobody enjoys paying taxes of any type because they don't experience immediate gratification and take for granted the many high standards of security, safety, cleanliness, and dependability of living in the United States. And I know of even fewer people who think very fondly of the IRS. And of course, many feel they are treated unfairly by the system that appears to them to penalize wealth. However, it is my belief that taxpayers who play by the rules will keep themselves at peace with the IRS.

As much as people resent paying taxes and how they are spent it is my experience that Americans continue to enjoy a high standard of living and more opportunities and freedoms than anywhere else, on average. Of course, we hear stories about billions of dollars being wasted but let's also feel grateful for living in a country that has progressed farther in about 200 years than any other country on the planet. Contemplate life without taxes all you want, but don't forget to also imagine life without a fire engine or police officer when you need them, clean and properly built highways and bridges, safe workplaces, clean and safe outdoor environments, healthy food and water, dependable power, disease prevention, the most massive and sophisticated military protection in the world, and exploration into the cutting edge of science and technology. If you wish to earn money and create wealth, paying taxes is part of the process.

Wisdom on Wealth

Tax revenue is an essential aspect of economies in the industrialized world. With the system as flexible as we have, however, and with some basic knowledge, you can maximize it to your benefit as much as possible.

Regarding audits, along with patience, bring your honesty, knowledge, and proof. Don't be intimidated by long forms. They can save you plenty of money and generally require only basic math. When taxes become too much of a hassle, don't start pulling your hair out. Hire a qualified professional. And be sure to use all the creative strategies available for tax savings if in business and in handling retirement funds and gifts.

CHAPTER 13

Enjoying Your Wealthy Later Years

Many people don't look forward to retirement because it conjures up images of old age, bad health, and boredom. Yet more than 26 percent of the U.S. population is now over the age of 50 and this segment of the population keeps growing.

Wisdom on Wealth

Most people will continue to be mentally and physically active for quite a number of years, especially those who have taken good care of themselves and stayed healthy.

While some choose to retire earlier, most working people will retire in their late 50s to mid-60s. Many people work to the age of 65 because this is presently the age at which workers are eligible for maximum benefits. As life expectancies increase and Social Security funding becomes more critical, this age at which workers are eligible for maximum benefits will change to age 67 for those born in 1960 or later. At age 62, workers get 80 percent of the maximum locked-in graduated upward small increments to 65, as long as they have earned enough work credits. If you are healthy and it appears that you will live for many more years and like your work, you may want to wait until you are eligible for full benefits. Receiving benefits for life at the 80-percent level for these extra years, however, may equal or exceed the total received by waiting until age 65.

Social Security benefits replace 42 percent of the average person's earnings. Those with lower incomes receive a higher percent and those with higher incomes receive a lower percent. For example, if you are 45 years old and have been earning $20,000 a year, you may receive about $900 a month at age 65, while if you are in the $50,000 bracket, your benefits will rise to about $1,470. Actual amounts vary, depending on your past and future earnings and the inflation rate. Call Social Security at 800-772-1213 to get a copy of your Personal Earnings and Benefit Statement and other information.

HOUSING

Throughout your life, comfortable housing will most likely be your greatest expense, whether it is just a couple of hundred dollars a month for taxes, insurance, and maintenance or up to several thousand dollars, including mortgage payments. Ideally, one should be *mortgage-free* by their 50s and beyond. Downsizing your housing is an option to consider in retirement if children have left the home.

In addition, as referred to in the chapter on housing, *where* you live has an immense effect on housing costs. This factor can be even more critical when you are living on a fixed income, which is the case for many retirees. You must ask yourself some basic questions:

- Do you prefer cold or warm climates?
- Do you wish to live in a rural, suburban, or city atmosphere?
- Do you want to be near your children or other relatives or friends, or near where you have memories of growing up?
- Do you require certain types of services that are more easily accessible in one area than another?
- Do you like the seashore, desert, mountains, prairie, or wetlands?
- How progressive do you expect an area to be?

With some compromising you can find a decent place to live out your retirement years happily. Several books offer advice on the best places to retire. Among them is *Retirement Places Rated* by D. Sagsavageau (McMillan), which offers some useful advice. But actually living in a community about a month or so before hauling all of your life's possessions across the country is the best way to assess your options. Generally, rural and Southern areas tend to have lower housing costs, as well as a lower cost of living, than other parts of the United States.

Also, there is the option to live abroad. Many countries offer very economical living conditions in pleasant climates with most of the amenities and services you want. An excellent book on this topic is *Travel and Retirement Edens Abroad* by Peter A. Dickinson (Little Brown & Co.). Many decide to leave the United States for tax reasons, but unless you give up U.S. citizenship you still are required to file a tax return. Should you not file, you won't get harassed outside the United States but don't expect a warm welcome trying to reestablish yourself, should you return. Many choose to file, because about $100,000 of income earned abroad per year is exempt from taxes for U.S. citizens, though different rules apply to investment income. And you may be liable for taxes in the country you relocate to. Another advantage may be the ability to obtain much cheaper medical care. However, if you require the same amenities you enjoy in this country, such as affordable and varied shopping opportunities, instant access to highly efficient communications, well-paved highways, and low crime, expect to pay about the same as you do in the United States to live.

Another option is a mobile home, which can be purchased or leased. Unlike buying a house, a mobile home won't appreciate in value. But the costs involved for a mobile home can be significantly less. Some retirees really thrive on traveling, in which case, a *motor* home can be the perfect option. If one place gets too hot or cold, or dull, you simply put your foot on the pedal. Although the costs of fuel and maintenance do add up somewhat, if you have sold your home and have at least a modest retirement income, this option can be quite affordable.

If you want to stay in one place for a while, most homes are parked in mobile/motor home parks where residents pay monthly fees ranging from about $80 up to several hundred dollars, depending on the area and services being offered. Another possibility is to park a mobile home on the property of your children subject to zoning laws and pay them a small fee to cover utility use that is drawn from their power outlets.

Perhaps after many years of living in your home, you finally have it all arranged exactly as you want and have minimal maintenance needs. If you are free of a mortgage, you should be able to pay others to assist you with your maintenance as needed, as well as travel, have hobbies, and participate in recreation. If you don't enjoy your money now, you never will.

If you can't afford to stay in your own home, here are a few alternatives:

- Share your home with another couple to free up some cash, especially if you do still have a mortgage.
- Build an addition to your children's home complete with its own kitchenette. Until comparatively recent times, families lived very near each other and helped out more in *actions* than with money. Although I love my privacy, I do believe there were some advantages to having a close, extended family. They built houses for each other, cared for children, and assisted with the ill and aging. Social Security, Medicare, and nursing homes did not exist and were rarely needed.
- Another way to stay in your home yet avoid maintenance costs is to sell the house to someone, such as your children, who will then lease it back to you at a rate that covers the mortgage and maintenance.
- Move to a condominium. In most condos, you pay a modest maintenance fee to keep the grounds proper and receive security, trash pickup, and other amenities.
- As a last resort, if you are cash strapped and have plenty of equity in your home, get a reverse mortgage that lets you gradually give up ownership of your home for monthly income to live on. To qualify, you must be at least 60 years of age and have the mortgage almost paid off.

STAY THRIFTY

Because you are now retired doesn't mean you should give up those thrifty habits. In fact, as a senior you are entitled to senior-citizen discounts on countless items from bread to airline tickets. Always ask when making purchases if senior discounts apply.

Have you got your will and other estate planning in order just as you want it? *Everyone* with assets they plan to pass on should have a will or a living trust, which can be more effective than a will in some cases. A typical will costs around $250. You can buy will kits and do some of the work yourself, which can save money, but you should still consult with a lawyer. The living trust normally permits most assets to pass directly to beneficiaries, bypassing probate. In addition to a living *trust*, I recommend having a living *will* that indicates to what extent

---

Wisdom on Wealth

Because you are now retired doesn't mean you should give up those thrifty habits. In fact, as a senior you are entitled to senior-citizen discounts on countless items from bread to airline tickets. Always ask when making purchases if senior discounts apply.

---

one wants artificial life support and heroic medical procedures performed to sustain one's existence.

MAKING FUNERAL ARRANGEMENTS

How do you wish your funeral to take place? You can leave written instructions to your descendants as to how extravagant you wish the ceremony to be, what type of casket, music, religious rituals you want, whether or not you want to be cremated (definitely a more economical alternative) and if so, where your ashes are to be scattered, or what cemetery you're to be buried in, and if you want your body to be donated to medical science. Though I tend to believe in placing your money in investments, the convenience of prepaid burial/funeral plans is something to consider to avoid putting this burden on others. A burial and funeral can cost from under $5,000 to well over $10,000, depending on the particulars. Forty-one states permit people to be their own funeral directors, in which you can deal directly with cemeteries and/or crematories to arrange for final disposition of a body including the paperwork. While practical and economical, however, handling burial arrangements in this manner may not be a responsibility you wish to bear during the mourning of a loved one. For further information on death arrangements, contact the Continental Association of Memorial Societies, 800-765-0107, and read *Caring for Your Own Dead* by Lisa Carlson, Upper Access Publishing, 1987, $12.95, and *Dealing Creatively with Death: A Manual of Death Education and Simple Burial* by Ernest Morgan, Barclay House, 1990, $11.95.

EARNING EXTRA INCOME

Some retirees still need or want to earn a little extra something. A number of the opportunities listed for young people in Chapter 4 can apply to seniors as well. Perhaps you can delve into some intriguing investment opportunity with your children. Remember that any income you earn beyond the limits set by Social Security will generate a dollar-for-dollar loss of your Social Security benefits until the age of 70. After 70, you can earn all you want while still collecting full benefits. You may want to use your skills on a part-time basis whether for teaching music or tennis, tax consulting, legal advice, writing, bicycle repair, or operating a small business from your home.

HANDLING YOUR INHERITANCE

Statistically speaking, everyone will outlive their parents. If your parents have followed through with appropriate estate planning, there is a strong chance you will have an inheritance upon their deaths or sooner, should they wish to give gifts while still alive. In most cases you are not able to accurately predict when deaths will occur and there are factors that can erode an estate, especially without proper planning.

Wisdom on Wealth

Regardless of your parents' financial status, *inheritance is not guaranteed.*

As adult children age and their parents approach the end of the average life span, it is natural for children to become more concerned about the financial logistics of inheritance. For the majority of people, this concern is not merely borne out of greed, as some parents may interpret it, but out of practical concern regarding financial planning. After all, if it is highly likely that you will inherit $25,000 in two years, your plans could be quite different than if you are more likely to inherit $250,000 in ten years. You might delay buying a house until you have a larger down payment or plan to pay off your mortgage early. Perhaps you will keep driving that old rattletrap a couple of years longer until you can buy a new car with cash. Maybe you have packed a child custodial account with a five-digit sum, postponing your grand trip to the Orient for the summer, in anticipation of sending your child to Harvard or Stanford. There are many practical reasons why you should understand all you can about the potential of your inheritance from both legal and financial standpoints.

Many parents are very private about their finances. They often feel that they have worked hard for much of their lives to get where they are financially and that their children should consider themselves lucky to get *anything* from them. Some seniors have the attitude of "I worked hard all my life, you should too" feeling that letting their children know about their possible inheritance may give them a disincentive to work and be productive. Others may feel a sense of jealousy toward their children as they realize the strong financial advantage it will afford them at a young age, while they worked and saved so many years. It is not uncommon to hear parents make remarks such as, "I'm almost 70 and still have a mortgage and you hope to pay off yours in your 30s?" or "I never got to Europe and you expect to spend a whole summer there?" or "I worked right up to the age of 65. What makes you think you are entitled to retire early?" It is not a matter of entitlement. It is a matter of *choices you make* to have whatever level of financial independence you want.

There are estimates that the parents of baby boomers (people now ages 35 to 50) collectively possess around $8 trillion in assets to pass along to the next generation. This averages to approximately $100,000 per inheritor. Because this amount of money is no small pocket change, it needs to be properly transferred and managed. However, if your parents should spend their last years cruising the world, staying in $300-a-night hotels, or investing their money at 3 percent when they could just as safely get 7 percent, *they have that right.*

Chances are that you are going to receive some amount of inheritance. Depending on the type of relationship you have with your parents, you may or may not be able to openly discuss inheritance. If they have not brought up the issue after you have aged through your twenties, it is clear that it is a topic they prefer not to discuss. If you are able to bring up the issue in a manner that is as little a reminder as possible of their mortality, you will have a greater chance. Nobody enjoys being reminded of their eventual death! You may inquire how they wish to spend their money during retirement. This approach may reduce your chances of your interest being interpreted as selfish. If they are receptive to it, see if they are knowledgeable of methods to save on estate taxes and have wills or living trusts. As is so true of many great conversations, they often arise as a result of an unexpected event. A time to discuss inheritance may be near the time of a tragedy of a close friend or family member. Deaths of those close to us may be a good trigger for such discussion, if it can be kept nonemotional. If parents are comfortable talking about inheritance, be prepared to tell them what would suit you best. Do *your* children need more funds for their college education? Do you want to start or expand a business? Or do you need a new car? Another method to reduce emotions is to have a third, unrelated party participate in the discussion.

Be alert to IRS rules regarding gift taxes and estate taxes if an inheritance exceeds $600,000. One popular way around some of these taxes is for parents to loan money to their children and then forgive the loan. Be able to document that all the proper loan-approval procedures were followed and market interest rates were charged. The only gifts excluded from the gift tax beyond $10,000 a year are for education and/or medical expenses.

As already emphasized, assume you are not going to inherit a nickel, so you won't be surprised if you don't. On the other hand, if the prospects look rather promising, don't stay in the dark. Learn what you can and try to have open and honest discussions about it. Every family has their own unique manner of communicating, so there is no advice that suits all situations. What appears fair to one family may not to another.

EPILOGUE

This book has been written for people who want to learn how to become *financially healthier* through a greater understanding of how and why our emotions are so tied to money, how to enjoy and relax with money, how to become conscious of different choices we have in controlling money, and how to pass this knowledge on to others.

There is an enormous amount of variation in how all of us enter into life and an equal variation in how we view the potential of money. The desire for more money than one now has is an integral part of human emotions. Without it, we would be missing a critical aspect of what drives us to get out of bed each day and be productive. More money means different things to many people.

For example, recently a coworker of mine asked me if I will buy a Mercedes if this book sells well. I said I had a comfortable car already but the one luxury I want is to one day travel around the world. Her response was "but you won't come back to a Mercedes!" Desire for more is only a problem when it becomes an obsession and can't seem to ever be fulfilled, leaving you in an endless cycle of assuming "if only I had this, everything would be fine." Only when we can give ourselves admiration for our positive attributes and come to peaceful terms with our relationship to money will long-term fulfillment be possible.

INDEX

3251